THE RISE OF THE WESTERN WORLD

THE RISE OF THE WESTERN WORLD

A New Economic History

DOUGLASS C. NORTH AND
ROBERT PAUL THOMAS

CAMBRIDGE
at the University Press · 1973

Published by the Syndics of the Cambridge University Press
Bentley House, 200 Euston Road, London NW1 2DB
American Branch: 32 East 57th Street, New York, N.Y. 10022

Library of Congress Catalog Card Number: 73-77258

ISBN: 0 521 20171 3

Composed in Great Britain by
Cox & Wyman Ltd
Norwich Street, Fakenham, Norfolk
Printed in the United States of America

CONTENTS

PREFACE

In some respects this is intended to be a revolutionary book, but in other respects it is very traditional indeed. It is revolutionary in that we have developed a comprehensive analytical framework to examine and explain the rise of the Western world; a framework consistent with and complementary to standard neo-classical economic theory. Since the book is written to be understandable (and hopefully interesting) for those without prior economic training, we have avoided the jargon of the profession and attempted to be as clear and as straightforward as possible.

This book is traditional in that we have built upon the pioneering studies of a host of predecessors. Scholars in the field will readily recognize our debt to Marc Bloch, Carlo Cipolla, Maurice Dobb, John U. Nef, M. M. Postan, Joseph Schumpeter, as well as the classic legal and constitutional studies of Pollock and Maitland and Stubbs.

We should emphasize that this is an interpretive study – an extended explanation sketch – rather than an economic history in the traditional sense. It provides neither the detailed and exhaustive study of standard economic history nor the precise and empirical tests of the new economic history. Its objective is to suggest new paths for the study of European economic history rather than fit either of these standard formats. It is more than anything an agenda for new research.

Our specific debts are many: to our long suffering colleagues and particularly Steven Cheung who provided assistance in developing the theoretical framework; to Martin Wolf for lending us the manuscript draft of his forthcoming book on French fiscal history; to David Herlihy and M. M. Postan who generously read and provided detailed suggestions and criticisms of earlier drafts of Parts One and Two; to Terry Anderson and Clyde Reed who provided both valuable research assistance as well as helpful critical comments; and finally to numerous audiences at various universities who heard earlier drafts of the theoretical issues. Ultimately, however, we are responsible for the book's shortcomings, although whatever value it has should be far more widely shared.

The National Science Foundation provided the financial support for research which made this book possible. We gratefully acknowledge our indebtedness for the continuing interest and support of the Foundation.

A special thanks is due to Marion Impola who has managed to translate our complicated and conflicting prose into readable and literate form, also to Joanne Olson for similar efforts.

At the risk of offending some scholars we have felt that the continuity and readability of the book could be improved by having a general list of sources for each chapter at the end of the book and confining the footnotes to citations that refer to direct quotations or involve explanatory asides.

PART ONE
THEORY AND OVERVIEW

1. THE ISSUE

The affluence of Western man is a new and unique phenomenon. In the past several centuries he has broken loose from the shackles of a world bound by abject poverty and recurring famine and has realized a quality of life which is made possible only by relative abundance. This book explains that unique historical achievement, the rise of the Western World.

Our arguments central to this book are straightforward. Efficient economic organization is the key to growth; the development of an efficient economic organization in Western Europe accounts for the rise of the West.

Efficient organization entails the establishment of institutional arrangements and property rights that create an incentive to channel individual economic effort into activities that bring the private rate of return close to the social rate of return.[1] In subsequent chapters we shall develop and apply a relevant model and then describe the parameter shifts which induce the institutional change. But first we must set out, in simplified form, the essential conditions for achieving economic growth and examine the difference between private and social costs and benefits.

In speaking of economic growth, we refer to a *per capita* long-run rise in income. True economic growth thus implies that the total income of society must increase more rapidly than population. A stationary state, on the other hand, produces no sustained rise in *per capita* income even though average income may rise and fall during cycles of quite long duration.

A stationary state will result when there is no inducement for individuals in the society to undertake those activities that lead to economic growth. Granted that individuals in the society may choose to ignore such positive incentives, and that in all societies some are content with their present situation; yet casual empiricism suggests that most people prefer more goods to fewer goods and act accordingly. Economic growth requires only that some part of the populace be acquisitive.

We therefore fall back on the explanation that if a society does not grow

---

[1] The private rate of return is the sum of the net receipts which the economic unit receives from undertaking an activity. The social rate of return is the total net benefit (positive or negative) that society gains from the same activity. It is the private rate of return plus the net effect of the activity upon everyone else in the society.

it is because no incentives are provided for economic initiative. Let us examine what this means. First we must isolate the type of growth of income which results from increases in the inputs of productive factors (land, labor, capital). Such direct increments lead to overall (extensive) growth but not necessarily to increases in income per person. Two situations can precipitate the latter sort of *per capita* improvement which we designate as true economic growth. On the one hand, the actual quantities of the *per capita* factors of production may increase. On the other, an increase in efficiency on the part of one or more of the factors of production will result in growth. Such increase of productivity can come about through realization of economies of scale, because of improvements in the quality of the factors of production (better educated labor, capital embodying new technology), or because of a reduction in those market imperfections that result from uncertainty and information costs, or as a result of organizational changes that remove market imperfections.

In the past, most economic historians have heralded technological change as the major source of Western economic growth; indeed European economic history pivots around the industrial revolution. More recently, others have stressed investment in human capital as the major source of growth. Still more currently, scholars have begun to explore the growth effects of the reduction in costs of market information. There can be no doubt that each of these elements has contributed notably to growth in output. So have economies of scale, based on production for larger and larger markets. For that reason, and since we are concerned entirely with growth *per capita*, the expansion of population itself adds still another dimension to our determination of 'true' economic growth.

The previous paragraph reflects what economic historians and economists have almost universally cited as determinants of economic growth in their diagnoses of the past performance of economies. Yet the explanation clearly has a hole in it. We are left wondering: if all that is required for economic growth is investment and innovation, why have some societies missed this desirable outcome?

The answer, we contend, brings us back to the original thesis. The factors we have listed (innovation, economies of scale, education, capital accumulation, etc.) are not causes of growth; they *are* growth. This book focuses on what causes economic growth. Growth will simply not occur unless the existing economic organization is efficient. Individuals must be lured by incentives to undertake the socially desirable activities. Some mechanism must be devised to bring social and private rates of return into closer parity. Private benefits or costs are the gains or losses to an individual participant in any economic transaction. Social costs or benefits are those affecting the whole society. A discrepancy between private and social benefits or costs means that some third party or parties, without their consent, will receive some of the benefits or incur some of the costs. Such a difference occurs whenever property rights are poorly defined, or are not enforced. If the private costs exceed the private benefits, individuals ordinarily will not be willing to undertake the activity even though it is socially profitable. Some of the historical issues to be dealt with in this book illustrate each of the situations with regard to property rights.

Take the case of ocean shipping and international trade. A major obstacle to its development was the inability of navigators to determine their true location. This requires a knowledge of two co-ordinates: latitude and longitude. The ability to determine latitude was early discovered and only required measuring the altitude of the Pole star; but in southern latitudes this lies below the horizon. Searching for a substitute method, Prince Henry of Portugal convened a group of mathematical experts who discovered that the determination of meridian solar altitude, when coupled with tables of the sun's declination, could yield the needed information on latitude. The determination of longitude, however, was more difficult since it required a timepiece which would remain accurate for the duration of long ocean voyages. Phillip II of Spain first offered a prize of 1000 crowns for the invention of such a timepiece. Holland raised the prize to 100,000 florins, and the British finally offered a prize ranging from £10,000 to £20,000 depending on the chronometer's accuracy. This prize hung in suspension until the eighteenth century when it was finally won by John Harrison, who devoted the greater part of his lifetime to the solution. The benefits to society of accurately determining a ship's position were immense in terms of reducing ship losses and lowering the costs of trade. How much sooner might the breakthrough have occurred, had there been property rights to assure an inventor some of the increased income resultant on the saving of ships and time? (He would also, of course, have had to bear the high costs of research and the uncertainty of finding a solution.) The payments to mathematicians and the proferred prizes were artificial devices to stimulate effort, whereas a more general incentive could have been provided by a law assigning exclusive rights to intellectual property including new ideas, inventions, and innovations. In the absence of such property rights, few would risk private resources for social gains.

As to means of enforcing property rights, this too can be illustrated by the case of ocean shipping. For centuries pirates and privateers were unwelcome but ubiquitous beneficiaries of trade. The threat of piracy raised the costs of commerce and reduced its extent. One solution was to pay bribes, and the English forestalled the depredations of North African pirates in the Mediterranean for many years by that forthright tactic. Bribery was 'efficient' because the income gains from trading freely in the Mediterranean were sufficiently greater than the bribes to leave the nation better off, on balance, and the solution was for a time less expensive than naval protection.

Other nations during this era protected shipping by convoy, while still others deployed naval squadrons. Ultimately piracy disappeared because of the international enforcement of property rights by navies.

Our third illustration, dealing with imperfectly stipulated property rights, comes from land policy in early modern Spain. As land became scarce with growing population, the social rate of return on improving the efficiency of agriculture rose, but the private return did not, because the Crown had previously granted to the shepherds' guild (the Mesta) exclusive rights to drive their sheep across Spain in their accustomed manner. A landowner who carefully prepared and grew a crop might expect at any moment to have it eaten or trampled by flocks of migrating sheep. In this case the ostensible owner did not have exclusive rights to his land.

These illustrations probably will have raised more questions than solutions for the curious reader. Why didn't societies develop property rights over intellectual property earlier? Why were pirates ever allowed headway? Why didn't the king of Spain abrogate the privileges of the Mesta and permit fee-simple absolute ownership of land?

In the first example, two possible answers occur. Either no way had been devised to make each shipowner pay to the inventor his share of the gains from increased safety at sea (a 'technological' limitation), or it appeared at the time that the costs of collection would exceed the benefits to be expected from a potential invention.

In the second case, bribery was initially better than piracy since the nation profited even after making the payment. Convoying was frequently found to be a still better solution. However, with the expansion of trade it ultimately became evident that the complete elimination of piracy was the cheapest alternative.

In answer to the third question, the king of Spain derived a substantial part of his revenue from the Mesta, and it was not clear that he could gain from abrogating their rights. Although the income of society would have been increased by such a change, it would appear that the Crown's own revenue from land taxes, reduced by the costs of reorganizing property rights and collecting the levies, would not, at least in the short run, have equalled the traditional revenues from the Mesta. Might the beleaguered property owners then have followed British policy by bribing the shepherds not to cross their lands? The difficulty here is the 'free-rider' problem of economics. Rallying all property owners to support such a project would involve costs greater than the expected benefits, since each individual would avoid contributing to the bribe, hoping to benefit from the contributions of all the others.

We then discover two general reasons why, historically, property rights have not evolved to bring private returns into parity with social returns. (1) Technique may be lacking to counteract the free-rider and/or to compel third parties to bear their share of the costs of a transaction. For example, the costs of protecting individual overland traders from depredations by lords ensconced in castles overlooking the routes originally made it cheaper to bribe or pay tolls than to attempt to circumvent them, but the advent of gunpowder and the cannon eventually made such fortresses vulnerable and reduced the costs of enforcing these property rights. Right to the present day, technical problems have made it similarly difficult, and therefore costly, to develop and enforce property rights in ideas, inventions, and innovations and in some natural resources like air and water. To bring the private return closer to the social return, secrecy, rewards, prizes, copyrights and patent laws have been devised at various times; but the techniques of excluding outsiders from the benefits continue to this day to remain costly and imperfect.

(2) The costs of creating or enforcing property rights may exceed the benefits to any group or individual. The illustrations above provide cases in point. The losses from pirates or privateers may have been less than the costs of convoying or of naval attack. Similarly, in abrogating the Mesta's privileges, establishing private property in land, and enacting taxes on its income, the king of Spain would have faced not only the uncertainty of the ultimate revenue, but known costs of reorganization and collection, that exceeded the gains of undertaking such reforms.

If exclusiveness and the enforcement of accompanying property rights could be freely assured – that is, in the absence of transactions costs – the achievement of growth would be simple indeed. Everyone would reap the benefits or bear the costs of his actions. If the innovation of new techniques, methods or organizational improvements to increase output imposed costs on others, the innovator could, indeed must, compensate the losers. If he could do this and still be better off, it would be a true social improvement. However, once we return to the real world of positive transactions costs, the problems of achieving growth are more complicated, and they become still more uncertain when we recognize that adjustments must inevitably occur between the initial creation of a set of property rights and the operation of the system once those rights have been established. Property rights are always embedded in the institutional structure of a society, and the creation of new property rights demands new institutional arrangements to define and specify the way by which economic units can co-operate and compete.

We shall be particularly interested in those institutional arrangements which enable units to realize economies of scale (joint stock companies, corporations), to encourage innovation (prizes, patent laws), to improve the efficiency of factor markets (enclosures, bills of exchange, the abolition of

5

serfdom), or to reduce market imperfections (insurance companies). Such institutional arrangements have served to increase efficiency. Some could be created without changing existing property rights, others involved the creation of new property rights; some were accomplished by government, others by voluntary organization.

The establishment of organization, whether governmental or voluntary, involves real costs. These tend to vary directly with the number of participants who must be brought into agreement. In the case of the voluntary organizations, withdrawal is also voluntary, but in the case of governmental organization, withdrawal can be accomplished only by migration outside the political unit. That is, a partner in a joint stock company who comes to disagree with its policies can sell his partnership and form a new joint stock company; but if he joins with others in enacting a zoning ordinance, the uses to which he can put his property are restricted, and he is not at liberty to withdraw from its provisions so long as he holds that property, or he must change the law – itself a costly proposition.

In view of such real costs, new institutional arrangements will not be set up unless the private benefits of their creation promise to exceed the costs. We should note right away two important aspects to this formulation. (1) Devising new institutional arrangements takes time, thought and effort (i.e., it is costly) but since everyone can copy the new institutional form without compensating the individual(s) who devised the new arrangement, there will be a substantial difference between private and social benefits and costs; (2) governmental solutions entail the additional cost of being stuck with the decision in the future – that is, withdrawal costs are higher than those related to voluntary organizations. Both these caveats lead us to a further discussion of government and its role in economic organization.

We can, as a first approximation, view government simply as an organization that provides protection and justice in return for revenue. That is, we pay government to establish and enforce property rights. While we can envisage that voluntary groups might protect property rights on a narrow scale, it would be hard to imagine a generalized enforcement without governmental authority. Consider the reason. Ever since nomadism gave way to agricultural settlements, man has found two ways to acquire goods and services. He could produce them, on the one hand, or steal them from someone else on the other. In the latter case, coercion was a tool to redistribute wealth and income. Threatened by marauders, the producers of goods and services responded by investing in military defense. But the building of a fortress and the enlistment of soldiers immediately raised the specter of the free-rider. Since the fortress and troops could hardly protect some villagers without protecting all, it was to each man's advantage to let his neighbor do the paying if contributions were on a voluntary basis. Thus

6

defense, as a classic case of a public good,[2] involves the problem of excluding third parties from the benefits. The most effective solution was, and continues to be, the forming of governmental authorities and taxing of all beneficiaries.

Justice and the enforcement of property rights are simply another example of a public good publicly funded. These requisites of an ordered society are typically embodied in a set of written or unwritten rules of the game. The customs of the manor, which we shall examine in the context of the medieval world, prevailed by precedent alone; written constitutions have evolved more recently. But historically such arrangements have roamed the whole spectrum from the most rudimentary (in which an absolutist ruler prevails) to detailed constitutions with clear separation of powers such as that created in 1787 in Philadelphia. These fundamental institutions reduce uncertainty by providing the basic ground rules underlying the specific or secondary institutional arrangements, which are the particular laws, rules and customs of a society.

In general, we shall observe that governments were able to define and enforce property rights at a lower cost than could voluntary groups, and that these gains became even more pronounced as markets expanded. Therefore, voluntary groups had an incentive (additional to the 'free-rider' problem) to trade revenue (taxes) in return for the rigorous definition and enforcement of property rights by government.

However, there is no guarantee that the government will find it to be in its interest to protect those property rights which encourage efficiency (i.e., raise the private rates of return on economic activities towards the social rate) as against those in which the property rights protected may thwart growth altogether. We have already seen an instance of this in the case of the Spanish Mesta. As a parallel, a prince may find short-run advantage in selling exclusive monopoly rights which may thwart innovation and factor mobility (and, therefore, growth) because he can obtain more revenue immediately from such a sale than from any other source – that is, the transaction costs of reorganizing the economic structure would exceed the immediate benefits. We shall explore the theoretical aspects of this issue in Chapter 8, since the differential success of European economies after the demise of feudalism depended on the relationships between the nation state's fiscal policy and property rights. We shall have prior occasion to explore the gradual evolution of the tax structure in the earlier years (thirteenth to fifteenth centuries) since the origins of the nation state and its pressing fiscal dilemma are to be found in those centuries.

---

[2] A public good is one which, once produced, people cannot be excluded from enjoying. If you protect a village, for example, you cannot avoid protecting all the villagers. Knowing this, each villager has an incentive to avoid paying for the village's defense. This situation is known as the free-rider problem.

Let us summarize what has been said. Economic growth occurs if output grows faster than population. Given the described assumptions about the way people behave, economic growth will occur if property rights make it worthwhile to undertake socially productive activity. The creating, specifying and enacting of such property rights are costly, in a degree affected by the state of technology and organization. As the potential grows for private gains to exceed transaction costs, efforts will be made to establish such property rights. Governments take over the protection and enforcement of property rights because they can do so at a lower cost than private volunteer groups. However, the fiscal needs of government may induce the protection of certain property rights which hinder rather than promote growth; therefore we have no guarantee that productive institutional arrangements will emerge.

We have yet to answer the question why property rights which cannot profitably be established at one point in time will later be economically justified. Obviously the benefits from developing new institutions and property rights must have risen relative to costs so that it became profitable to innovate. Therefore an analysis of those parameters which influence the relationships between benefits and costs becomes critical to our study. The predominant parameter shift which induced the institutional innovations that account for the rise of the Western World was population growth. Let us see how it worked historically.

2. AN OVERVIEW

We must step into history at some moment of time and in the process do violence to its essential continuity. We choose the tenth century – following the decay of the Carolingian Empire, when feudalism and manorialism shaped the society of much of Western Europe. Since the key to our story is the evolution of institutional arrangements it is worthwhile to describe feudalism as precisely but as accurately as possible by way of the following exposition from the *Shorter Cambridge Medieval History*, pp. 418–19.

> Although full-grown feudalism was largely the result of the breakdown of older government and law, it both inherited law from the past and created it by a rapid growth of custom based on present fact. In one sense it may be defined as an arrangement of society based on contract, expressed or implied. The status of a person depended in every way on his position on the land, and on the other hand land-tenure determined political rights and duties. The acts constituting the feudal contract were called *homage* and *investiture*. The tenant or vassal knelt before the lord surrounded by his court (*curia*), placing his folded hands between those of the lord, and thus became his 'man' (*homme*, whence the word homage). He also took an oath of fealty (*fidelitas*) of special obligation. This of course was the ancient ceremony of commendation developed and specialized. The lord in his turn responded by 'investiture', handing to his vassal a banner, a staff, a clod of earth, a charter, or other symbol of the property or office conceded, the *fief* (*feodum* or *Lehn*) as it was termed, while the older word *benefice* went gradually out of use. This was the free and honourable tenure characterized by military service, but the peasant, whether free or serf, equally swore a form of fealty and was invested with the tenement he held of his lord. The feudal nexus thus created essentially involved reciprocity.

Economic activity, however, centered around the manor, and again the *Shorter Cambridge Medieval History* provides for the complexity of this institution a concise description, pp. 424–5.

The most characteristic version of the manorial village, although narrowest in its distribution, was the English 'manor', which became the most closely organized and most durable of the type. It consisted of two once distinct elements, the economic and the administrative, and thus strove towards two intimately connected aims, the subsistence of the villagers, and the lord's profit and authority. The village community lay at the basis of the whole. In a brief description only an average account, subject to countless irregularities, can be given. The normal villager (*villanus villein*) would hold a *yardland* or *virgate* of thirty acres (or its half, a *bovate*), distributed in scattered acre-strips in the three or two open fields of the manor, which might coincide with the village or be only a part of it. He followed the manor routine (its 'custom') in the cultivation, the ploughing, sowing, and reaping, of his strips; independent husbandry was barely possible in the open fields. In each year one field in rotation out of the two or three (as the case might be) was left fallow and unenclosed for beasts to graze in; the cultivated field or fields were fenced round. His own livestock up to a stated number were free to pasture in the 'waste'; he had his share of the hay-meadow. Intermingled with the tenants' strips in the open fields lay the strips kept by the lord of the manor in his own hands, his *demesne*. There was a strong tendency, however, to isolate the demesne in a home-farm. In this connexion arose the greater part of the labour services which the villager owed for his tenement. Each villein household owed *week-work* (one labourer) of usually three days a week on the demesne farm, which included its share of the ploughs, oxen, and implements for all kinds of work and cartage. The *cottars*, whose holdings were much smaller, owed of course less labour. At the peak periods of mowing and reaping, *boon-work* of all kinds was required in addition, and in this the freemen, socagers and others, who occupied their tenements for a rent or other terms implying free contract, took their part. A freeman, however, might hold land on villein tenure, and *vice versa*. The *assarts*, or reclamations from the waste, were commonly less burdened with the heavy dues of villeinage. Dues of all kinds, indeed, pressed on both villein and freeman of the manor, render of hens, eggs, special payments, etc. The villein, besides being tied to the soil, was subject to the servile fine of *merchet* (*formariage*) on his daughter's marriage and to the exaction of his best beast as heriot (*mainmorte*) on his death; he paid the money levy of tallage at the lord's will; his corn was ground in the lord's mill; in France the lord's oven and his winepress were seigneurial monopolies. The villein might be selected as reeve or other petty official of rural manorial economy. His condition, however, was mitigated by the growth of the custom of the manor, which at any rate fixed the exactions he laboured under and secured him in his hereditary holding. Like the freeman he attended the manorial court, which declared the custom of the manor and its working. The lord of many manors would send round steward or bailiff to receive his profits and collect produce for his support in those in which he periodically resided. Besides the subsistence of the villagers, in short, their labour was to provide that of the warrior governing class and the allied ecclesiastical dignitaries, to both of whom they owed as a rule what little peace, justice, and enlightenment they had.

Thus the customs of the manor became the unwritten 'constitution', or the fundamental institutional arrangement of an essentially anarchic world, most properly viewed as small isolated settlements, frequently in the lee of a fortified place and surrounded by wilderness. The wooden or earth castle, the knight, and the relatively self-sufficient manor had emerged as the most viable response to the collapse of order and the recurrent invasions of Norsemen, Moslems, and Magyars. While the terror of foreign marauders had declined by the middle of the tenth century, the land seethed with continual warfare and brigandage, as the power of local lords waxed and waned. Feudalism provided a measure of stability and order in this fragmented world. Where security prevailed, population began once more to increase. If growing numbers threatened to crowd a manor uncomfortably, there was always new land to be cleared and cultivated within the protection of a new lord. Spreading out north and west over Europe, the waves of migrants gradually engulfed the wilderness, leaving less space for brigands to hide and bringing more and more area under the protection of lords and their vassals. True, they fought amongst themselves; but gradually, very gradually, the chaos gave way, the strife declined.

Commerce between different parts of Europe had always been potentially of mutual benefit, since the variety of resources and climatic conditions induced differentiation of crops and livestock. But trade had been sporadic because so many dangers within the wilderness beset the traveling merchant. As peace and security now revived, so did the profitability of exchanging varied products. In response, towns were taking form in the more densely settled areas either under the protection of a lord or as independent entities with their own walls, government, and military defense. Here skills and crafts flourished, providing 'manufactured' goods to trade for the needed food and raw materials from the countryside.

Such a shift away from self-sufficiency toward more specialization and increasing trade undermined the efficiency of the old feudal and manorial relationship. Where the great lords had once been happy to claim the defensive services of a number of knights for forty days a year from their vassals, they now chose to receive a money payment (*scutage*) which enabled them to hire mercenary troops as needed. The vassal too could specialize with more efficiency when freed of the stringent requirement of armed labor services. On the manor, both lord and serf gained flexibility in consumption and transactions when a money payment (*commutation*) replaced labor services.

The revival of trade and commerce in the eleventh and twelfth centuries led not only to the proliferation of towns but to a host of institutional arrangements designed to reduce market imperfections. As new towns developed their own governments for administration and protection, they necessarily evolved bodies of law to adjudicate disputes arising from these new conditions. The towns of northern Italy, central Germany, and Flanders became thriving centers of commerce, as population and trade continued to grow.

But by the thirteenth century a change was becoming evident. The best land had all been taken up, and new settlement now had to rely on poorer quality land or work the existing cultivated land more intensively. A young laborer could no longer produce as much as did his forebears because he could not command as much land. Prices for those goods which it required a great deal of land to produce – agricultural products – rose relative to other goods. In contrast, since labor had grown relatively more abundant, labor-intensive goods fell in price relative to land-intensive goods. The customary feudal and manorial contractual arrangements, already altered by trade and by the growth of a money economy, now met further incentive for change. Since land had become much more valuable, both lord and peasant had reason to seek more exclusive use of land and to place more restrictions on its use by others. Similarly, because he now produced relatively less, the earnings of the peasant laborer declined. The customs of the manor limited the changes that could be made, but these new conditions did lead to efforts to modify existing contractual arrangements to permit more exclusive use of land. The new economic conditions gave the lord greater 'bargaining' strength in negotiating new contractual arrangements with the serf. The effect of a relative increase in the quantity of labor, predictably, was a fall in the living standard of the worker. Food became more expensive. Real earnings declined.

While the thirteenth century witnessed an inexorable decline in the standard of life of the peasant, it unfolded a pageant of expansion in trade and commerce. Led by Venice, Italian cities stretched their trade routes throughout the Mediterranean and reached ever farther along the Atlantic Coast, even to Britain. The Champagne Fair in France, the Flemish wool trade, and the German mining and commercial centers all participated in a growing commerce which induced improvements in banking and commercial institutional arrangements.

Throughout the century, because of diminishing returns to labor in agriculture, population growth continued to outstrip the growth in output. The first evident consequence was the widespread famine of 1315–17. But far more deadly and persistent was the plague, both bubonic and pneumonic, which spread over Europe between 1347 and 1351. Thereafter, the pestilence became endemic, and successive epidemics continued to decimate towns and countryside.

No accurate figures cite the extent of the population decline, but it appears to have continued for a century. The result was a reversal in relative product and factor values. Once again land had become relatively abundant and labor scarcer and more valuable. The marginal lands everywhere went out of production, and some land was shifted away from crops to the raising of livestock which requires larger expanses of land. Real wages rose everywhere in spite of political efforts to curb them. For the first time, rudimentary statistics begin to emerge to show the economic conditions that prevailed.[1] Based on them, Fig. 2.1 pictures the period's relative decline in agricultural prices, the rise in wages, and the consequent rise in real wages.

Falling rents made the landlord worse off at the same time that the scarcity of labor improved the bargaining strength of the worker. Under this influence the master–servant aspect of manorialism gradually fell away. Leases were lengthened, and the villein began to acquire exclusive rights to his land. Only where the lords could effectively collude rather than compete for labor, as in Eastern Europe, could they thwart the changing status (and income) of their former vassals.

While the bonds of manorialism were dissolving in the countryside, the same force of declining population was adversely affecting trade and commerce. Contracting markets lessened the incentive to reduce market imperfections. With the exception of Italian banking, where the great Medici bank in Florence was flourishing, the institutional arrangements now being devised were more 'defensive' in nature, designed chiefly to maintain existing markets, to monopolize trade, and to prevent entry (and competition). The Hanseatic League, a group of trading cities, appears to have been such a defensive arrangement on an international level, and the rise of craft guilds in towns reflected the same trend locally.

By the time that population again began to grow in the last half of the fifteenth century, the basic structure of a feudal society had given way. Its erosion was to be completed by the next cycle of population expansion and Malthusian pressure on resources. Figs. 2.2 and 2.3 show the contours of rising agricultural prices and falling real wages in the sixteenth century which in these respects replicated the thirteenth. But crucial differences now appeared. Improvements in ships and navigation led to explorations

---

[1] We would caution the reader that not only are the quantitative data sparse and of uneven quality but usually they relate to a narrow geographic area. We have used the data primarily as illustrative of broad trends over larger geographic units when we feel confident that such quantitative information does in fact mirror more general tendencies.

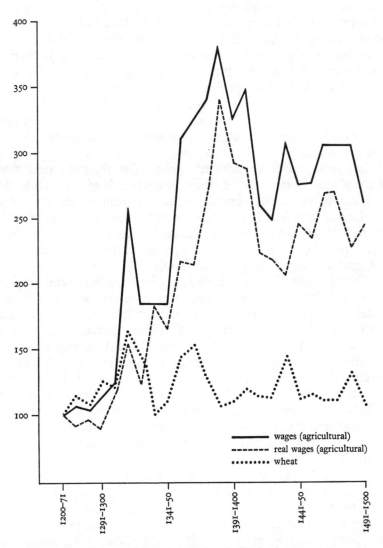

Fig. 2.1.   The wages of labor and the price of wheat in England: 1200–1500.
   Sources: wheat, J. E. Thorold Rogers, *A History of Agriculture and Prices in England: 1261–1400*, vol. 1 (1400–1500), p. 245, vol. 4, p. 292; wages, Lord Beveridge, 'Westminster Wages in the Manorial Era', *The Economic History Review*, 8, no. 1 (August 1955). Note: missing observations were filled by interpolation.

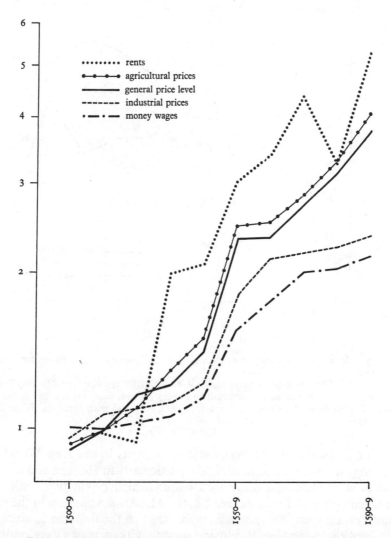

Fig. 2.2. Indices of rents, agricultural prices, the general price level, industrial prices and money wages for England: 1500–1600.

Sources: Joan Thirsk, *The Agrarian History of England and Wales*, vol. 4, 1500–1640 (Cambridge University Press, 1967), pp. 862, 865; Eric Kerridge, 'The Movement of Rent, 1540–1640', *The Economic History Review*, 2nd series, 6 (August 1953), 25.

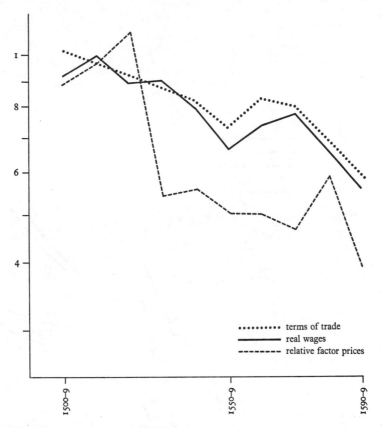

Fig. 2.3. Index of real wages, the terms of trade and relative factor prices for England: 1500–1600.

Sources: E. H. Phelps-Brown and Sheila V. Hopkins, 'Wage-Rates and Prices: Evidence for Population Pressure in the Sixteenth Century', *Economica*, 24, no. 96, p. 306; and 'Seven Centuries of the Prices of Consumables, Compared with Builders' Wage-Rates', *Economica*, 23, no. 92, pp. 311–14.

which culminated in discoveries and settlements in the New World. The evolving structure of property rights (particularly in Holland and England) became a fundamental framework within which productive institutional arrangements took form. As a result, the Malthusian reaction in the seventeenth century was far less catastrophic than in the fourteenth, since both immigration to the New World and productivity increases were mitigating the diminishing returns in agriculture.

But we have gone ahead of our story. Rising agricultural prices and the consequent more rapid rise in rents had led to renewed efforts to eliminate the vestiges of common ownership of land. England inaugurated an era of enclosures supported by basic statutes providing for easier transfer of property and protection of the peasant.

The sixteenth century was equally an age of commercial expansion. Trade was encouraged by the growing differentiation in factor endowments, since the lands of Eastern Europe were still abundant relative to population, whereas the burgeoning towns and cities of Western Europe had become centers of skilled trades and manufactures. Treasure from the New World, pouring in a silver flood through such cities as Lisbon, Cadiz, Bordeaux, Rouen, Antwerp, Amsterdam, Bristol and London, additionally nourished this growing international market. The consequence was the innovation and proliferation of a host of arrangements such as joint stock companies and institutions designed to reduce market imperfection by coping with problems of financing and risk. Another logical step then followed: a body of laws developed to provide more efficient property rights in the ownership and exchange of intangible assets.

To a modern reader this progression may sound inevitably simple. It was far from that. And in light of the previous chapter, one should be already prepared for the widely divergent experiments and false starts that in fact emerged during this period in different regions.

Basic to all other changes was the form of the evolving nation-state induced by the expanding market economy. In the fragmented world of feudal society, the fixed castle and the knight in armor had been the chessmen in the game of defense. As these gave way before new military technology (the crossbow, longbow, pike and gunpowder) the optimal size of the most efficient military unit gradually increased. The manor had to grow for efficiency into a community, a state; and, to survive, the state had to achieve far greater fiscal revenues than could be obtained from traditional feudal sources. Trade had to be encouraged, increased, extended, to bring in tax revenues to the head of state. And whereas the feudal castle had been unable to provide sufficient protection for long-distance trade, the larger political units or coalitions that emerged now were capable of sheltering more effectively the routes needed for the growth of commerce.

An increase in such trade became the overriding concern of every sovereign in Europe. Intrigues, coalition, betrayal, confiscations, treaties, ingenious and ingenuous tax impositions, all entered the patchwork of endeavors which transformed feudal society ultimately into the nation-states. And the sort of state that emerged was determined by the strength a monarch could exert in claiming the monopoly powers of government, which in turn left an imprint on the structure of the developing economy.

In France and Spain the monarchy gradually wrested power away from representative bodies and developed a system (and level) of taxation which promoted local and regional monopoly, stifled innovation and factor mobility, and led to a decline in productive economic activity which was relative in the case of France and absolute in the case of Spain.[2] In Holland, the changing conditions led to an oligarchy of merchants; in England, after years of strife, to the ascendancy of parliament over the Crown. And in both, to sustained economic growth, resulting from a hospitable environment for the evolution of a body of property rights which promoted institutional arrangements, leading to fee-simple absolute ownership in land, free labor, the protection of privately owned goods, patent laws and other encouragements to ownership of intellectual property, and a host of institutional arrangements to reduce market imperfections in product and capital markets.

Our story ends with the beginning of the eighteenth century. By then the essential conditions had been created for bringing the private rate of return close enough to the social rate, so that productivity increase was built into the system in Holland and England (as well as in the New World). Over the next century these conditions in these areas induced a revolution in technology which gradually spread over much of the rest of Europe and satellite colonies overseas as well.

[2] Because the price series varied between nations during the seventeenth century, we postpone our discussion of them to Chapter 9 below.

3. PROPERTY RIGHTS IN LAND AND MAN

Before we explore these six centuries in more detail, it is well to specify much more precisely the explanatory theory implicit in the previous chapters.

The pressure to change property rights emerges only as a resource becomes increasingly scarce relative to society's wants. In the world of the tenth century, at the point where we entered into it, land was abundant and therefore not worth the cost of devising exclusive rights to its use. When one piece of land was taken up, more was always available. Because the countryside lay under constant threat of ravage by marauding bands of Vikings, Moslems, Magyars or even of native brigands, greater value attached to any areas protected by a fortification and skilled soldiers. Such land, from the very beginning of the manorial system, was never a completely 'common-property' resource in the sense that economists use that phrase. Customs and precedents limited its usage to preclude overgrazing and other hazards implicit in common use.[1] We shall see later that manorial regulations grew more restrictive as land became scarce.

Two other basic elements entered into the manorial economy; the functions of protection, and the role of labor. In the matter of protection, the fortified castle and armored knights on horseback, having specialized skills in warfare, provided local security which could never be equalled by any group of peasants ill-armed with primitive weapons and lacking military skills. Moreover, against such an enemy as roving bands of raiders (whether by sea or land), a local lord and castle were more immediate and comforting a safeguard than a distant king and army. The chaos of the period, coupled with the character of military technology, made the feudal unit the efficient mode of protection. The lord and his knights, who specialized in producing protection and justice, depended on serfs for what they consumed. An alternative often pursued by the early Vikings, Magyars and Moslems

---

[1] In the case of a common-property resource each user has an incentive to exploit the resource without regard to other users, which results in a continual deterioration of the resource. Overgrazing of the land and overfishing of the seas are classic examples. Since no one owns the resource there is no incentive to conserve the resource or to improve efficiency in its use.

was to plunder the products of other communities' labor. But another method (and one which the Vikings themselves eventually adopted) was to contract for labor in their own vicinity by such arrangements as we have described in the previous chapter and shall shortly examine in greater detail.

The third element of the manorial economy, labor, involves an examination of the existing nature of property rights in man. Some might ask why in feudal times the lords did not simply make slaves of the peasants, owning them outright. For one reason, it was not difficult for an oppressed peasant to flee to a neighbouring castle where he might hope for a better bargain, since labor was scarce and lords were in competition for its use. Second, it would have been costly to direct and supervise slaves in the many types of tasks involved in making the self-sufficient manor a viable economic system.[2] In short, slavery was not the most efficient system when (1) the costs of enforcement were high, and (2) the costs of supervision were high relative to the alternative of serfdom. Under that alternative the villein was born to a status which he could not alter; but the institution of serfdom gained efficiency and avoided the need for much enforcement and supervision, since in exchange for a fixed amount of labor services to the lord to perform the variety of activities involved in the self-sufficient manorial economy, the serf was granted the rest of his time to produce for himself. It is true that the serf had an incentive to shirk when working the lord's land; but as we shall see later, this was at least partly countered by customs of the manor which explicitly or implicitly specified certain amounts of output per hour in the contractual arrangement and fines were levied for malfeasance.

Why did the lord require labor services rather than simply take a share of the serf's output? The answer is that there was no organized market for goods (and services). To have established the proper mix of goods owed and the implicit value to the lord of given goods at a given time would have involved lengthy and costly haggling, as variations in climate and other factors altered their relative availabilities. In the absence of an organized market to provide information on prices, both parties could do better by agreeing to produce the combination of goods they wanted by an exchange of the peasants' services for those of the lord. In cases where there was little variation over time in supply (like cordwood) or where the item was small or indivisible (such as a goose for a feast day) such arrangements were supplemented by the payment to the lord of some goods in kind. But the key to the contractual arrangement was labor services in return for the lord's protection; and in time this came to embrace justice through the

---

[2] If the lord had been producing one crop involving large-scale and repetitive operations (such as would be the case on a plantation for market production), then supervisory costs might have been low enough to make it economically feasible to hold slaves rather than serfs.

manorial court, as a natural adjunct.[3] The classic manor persisted as long as the initial conditions of chaos, abundant land, differential military endowments, and scarce labor prevailed.

Population growth upset this system and to examine what took place we must first indicate some of the determining factors of population size: that is factors affecting fertility and mortality.

Over man's history fertility has always tended to outstrip mortality, and population has grown despite the temporary setbacks of warfare, epidemic, famine and chaos. In purely economic terms, as long as good land was available so that additional people could produce as much as their forebears had, this trend continued. In the absence of war, mortality experience probably did not change very much over centuries of the Middle Ages except when crowding and declining living standards made the population susceptible to famine and more prone to communicable diseases such as the plague. While land was abundant, these economic checks tended to be short-run in character. In the terms introduced in Chapter 1, private benefits were high in bearing children, not only as a source of labor from a very early age, but as a source of social security in the extended family system that prevailed, whereby the able-bodied took care of the young and the aged. These gains outweighed the private costs (in terms of time and resource consumption) of rearing children. In short, when children were an asset, fertility rates tended to be very high, and in a world of abundant land, private and social benefits and costs were approximately equal. But as soon as all the good land was taken up and diminishing returns set in, private *versus* social costs and benefits suffered a sharp divergence.

It is clear that when diminishing returns forced a rise in the real cost of foodstuffs, and when the value of labor fell, the private cost of rearing a child also rose, and the private benefits (of his future labor) promptly fell. But the social costs had risen still more, because the additional child by adding to the total labor supply had contributed to a general decline in labor productivity caused by diminishing returns and had increased the relative overcrowding which hastened the spread of disease. It is true that the rise of private costs and the fall in private benefits would (and did) induce families to curtail fertility by such expedients as delayed marriages and primitive forms of contraception. But at the same time the divergence between private and social returns resulted in a fertility rate still too high for the society. We shall return to this point, but first let us look at the consequences of population growth in a region where land was yet abundant.

We have already noted that when the local manor became crowded to a

---

[3] A more theoretical analysis of the manorial system, written for the economist, is to be found in the authors' 'The Rise and Fall of the Manorial System: A Theoretical Model', *The Journal of Economic History*, 31, no. 4 (December 1971), 777–803.

point of diminishing returns, the overflow spread out into virgin areas. Settlers moving out over Northwest Europe encountered different soils and climates, and of necessity they set up varied patterns of agricultural activity. While adjacent manors might produce an almost identical mix of goods and services, the growing differentiation between regions increased the profitability in trading. In such an atmosphere towns revived (as in Italy) or developed (in Flanders) to turn their specialized skills into the production of 'manufactured' goods. The varied pattern of factor endowments (including human capital) thus enhanced the gains from trade and encouraged the extension of protection to commerce over larger areas than the local countryside. As a net result, then, population growth and colonization led to a growing diversity in factor endowments which in turn, by increasing the gains from trade, made it advantageous to extend the protection of property rights beyond the confines of the single manor. The spread of trade (and the concomitant use of money as the unit of account) altered the basic economic conditions which made the classic manor an efficient institutional arrangement.

Before the development of a viable market system, an agreement to share inputs had provided both lords and vassals with their desired consumption mixes at the lowest cost. But now that the market could be used to exchange goods and money could serve to measure the product, it clearly involved lower transaction costs to set up a system of wages, rents, or shares by contract. The manorial relationship had suffered an irreversible change, and although the 'customs of the manor' reduced the speed of transition, the lords and serfs, because a market existed, were increasingly willing to commute labor dues to money payments on an annual basis, and the lords to rent out their demesnes.

Meantime, as all of the best land was becoming settled, further growth in population had been pushing settlers to farming existing land more intensively or to moving to poorer land. In either case the relative value of land and labor had been changing, and this change would also exert a profound effect on the contractual arrangements and ultimately upon the fundamental institutional arrangements.

Take labor, to begin with. As we noted earlier, the value of an additional hour of labor would have fallen as productivity diminished, since the worker could produce less agricultural output per hour of work than his forebears. In effect the contractual arrangement between lord and villein had been altered. The labor services now produced less output on a *per capita* basis in return for the same amount of public goods – protection and justice. Even with great bargaining strength (since labor was now relatively abundant), the lord was limited in his ability to alter the contract in the short run by the customs of the manor. However, an annual commutation payment in lieu of labor services, its amount fixed by custom, would over time (and in the absence of inflation)[4] work to the lord's advantage. As a corollary, of course, the bargaining strength of the peasant was declining, so that over time the lord could also change the contractual arrangement to his favor (by demanding more labor time, goods in kind, or other bonuses).

Another predictable result of diminishing returns to labor input was that land was becoming scarce and rising in value; the exclusive right to a plot of land was ever more desirable as agricultural prices soared, and exclusive private property in land promised greater gains than ever before. We observed at the beginning of this chapter that even when land was abundant it was still relatively valuable when protected by proximity to the manor, so that even from early days some limitations had been set on the common-property aspects of such areas. As land scarcity now became general, the pressure to limit common-property uses increased, but the customs of the manor once more slowed down the changes that could be made in existing property rights. In this case, as in all the other parameter shifts we have discussed that resulted from population growth, the inherited structure of land use gave those who currently under the customary law had access to the land (but would be denied this access by exclusive ownership) an incentive to oppose the development of such property rights.

Given such a situation, we would not expect a once-and-for-all jump from common property to fee-simple private property: in terms of political and military strife the costs of abrogating the conflicting customs of the manor would have been prohibitive. Rather we would expect successive steps to reduce freedom of entry and to increase the degree of exclusiveness in land use. The opposition of the losers would be less drastic, and on occasion the gainers might find it feasible to 'pay off' the losers in order to acquire greater exclusive use. But remembering our caveat on political behavior in Chapter 1, the ultimate outcome would be uncertain.

The historical consequence of population growth, increasing land scarcity, and diminishing returns to a growing population in this period proved to be a fall in living standards to the point where famine and pestilence preyed on society, returning the cycle once more to a ratio of labor scarcity and land abundance. Again, all the signals were reversed. Under fundamental institutional arrangements inherited from the previous labor-abundant era, rents and the value of land would now fall and the incentive to further develop property rights in land would be countered by the urgent need to obtain property rights in man and his labor, as in our opening period. To the extent that lords could avoid competition for labor, they could prevent a rise in real wages, but collusion over an area large enough to be effective would require centralized political coercion. Where political

---

[4] We shall see, however, that the rise of the money economy did bring fluctuations in the general price level and that inflation in the thirteenth century forced the lord to adopt a different solution.

fragmentation or divided political power prevented such collusion, the peasant could gradually exact better terms and rising real wages, since his bargaining strength had improved.

Again, existing fundamental institutional arrangements, the customs of the manor, assured that the new secondary institutional arrangements would be piecemeal steps rather than a once-and-for-all jump to a 'free' labor force. By gradual steps the manorial lord and the peasant-servant would be transformed into employer and employee or landlord and tenant.

The decline in population also contracted markets and exchange and encouraged the revival of more self-sufficiency and the erection of barriers against outside competition to protect the markets that survived; the power of guilds grew and they exerted every effort to police and control entry into trades and prevent outside competition.

We have set the scene. Now, we explore in more detail what took place in these six centuries.

4. ECONOMIC CONDITIONS AT THE END OF THE EARLY MIDDLE AGES

That the Middle Ages were an unchanging economic plateau was once the prevailing opinion of historians. Along with its theoretical under-pinning, the stage theory of history, this view has now been consigned to the intellectual rubbish heap. Today's scholars generally agree that the period under consideration was a dynamically expanding era. Certainly from the eleventh century, if not before, commerce burgeoned, cities were founded and grew, and economic specialization came into its own.

During the important historical era of the high Middle Ages (1000–1300) the focus of the development of the Western World shifted once and for all from the classic lands of the Mediterranean to the plains of Northern Europe. To explain these phenomena satisfactorily has become one of the great historical quests, and the problem dominated the attention of the great historian Henri Pirenne. Although the Pirenne thesis has been all but disproved, the question he concentrated upon remains one of the great historial issues: Why did Northern Europe develop during the high Middle Ages to attain lasting dominance?

Labeling this development a commercial by-product of the crusades, which re-opened the Mediterranean Sea to trade, Pirenne saw the expansion of Northern Europe as the direct response to an external stimulus – the reaction of its inhabitants to the opportunity to reap gains from trade with other areas of the Mediterranean. The host of scholars who arose in opposition to Pirenne, after destroying his thesis in detail, have almost exclusively focused upon factors internal to the society of Northern Europe. The most widely accepted current explanation follows the traditional Marxian view that technological change was the disequilibrating force from which all else flowed. Most contemporary Marxist historians hold this opinion, and they are joined by many scholars who in other respects would consider themselves thoroughly anti-Marxist. The current view attributes the economic growth of the period to the cumulative effect of new inventions and systems which made available more animal, water, and wind power and allowed inputs to be combined more efficiently. Improved agricultural productivity, rather than the external stimulus of increased

Mediterranean commerce, is said to account for the rapid development of the region.

The Marxist interpretation, in our opinion, suffers from certain fatal flaws.[1] In its place we offer an alternative thesis which we feel is both better economics and more consistent with the historical evidence. In capsule form: we suggest that a growing population was the exogenous variable that basically accounts for the growth and development of Western Europe during the high Middle Ages. An expanding population in a local area would eventually encounter diminishing returns to further increases in the size of the labor force. Part of the increased labor force would as a consequence migrate to take up virgin land in the wilderness, thus extending the frontiers of settlement. However, the density of habitation would still be greater in the older areas than on the frontier, and this differential, resulting in a variation of land-to-labor ratios between areas, when coupled with regional differences in natural resource endowments, would lead to different types of production. Such variances would allow profitable exchanges of products between regions. We submit, therefore, that the development and expansion of a market economy during the Middle Ages was a direct response to the opportunity to gain from the specialization and trade made feasible by population growth. The growth in towns facilitated local and regional exchanges, and the expansion of these markets made it profitable to specialize functions, to introduce new technologies, and to adjust the production processes to altered conditions. In sum, a growing population created the basis for trade; the resulting expansion of the market economy caused the medieval economy to react, if slowly, precisely in the manner Adam Smith would have predicted. With this brief introduction to the Middle Ages, let us turn back to the ninth century.

I

Western Europe at the dawn of the ninth century can best be visualized as a vast wilderness thinly populated by Europeans living in family groups huddled together in clusters of small feudal villages, separated by expanses of natural vegetation. Except in Italy, cities as we now know them were almost non-existent. The villages comprised several peasant huts, a parish church, and a manor house, with all the necessary capital goods such as mills, presses, ovens and barns located near by. Generally, individual garden plots adjoined the huts. Radiating from the villages were large cultivated open fields; close by were expanses of pasture lands and wastelands still covered with natural vegetation.

---

[1] We shall have occasion to discuss these flaws below. See also the final footnote to our article, 'An Economic Theory of the Growth of the Western World', *The Economic History Review*, 2nd series, 22, no. 1 (1970), 1–17.

Over the small proportion of available land actually cultivated these villagers grew such cereal grains as wheat, rye, barley, and even some oats, out of which the basic foodstuff, bread, was made. The forests and wilds occupied a large role in the village economy; in addition to providing fuel and construction materials, and game and wild vegetation for the table, they offered pasture for sheep, cows, and – above all else – for swine. Herds of pigs, providing both meat and lard, roamed in every forest and were the mainstay of every village.

The arable fields were divided into contiguous parcels or strips, the rights to which were allotted between the lord and the peasants. The lord's land, known as the demesne, could be located among or apart from the peasants' open fields. Individual peasants held rights to strips located in almost random pattern throughout the field. The field was farmed co-operatively with community decisions made as to when to plough, plant and harvest, in a plan of agriculture known today as the open-field system.

The manor composed of one or more villages was headed by a seigneur or lord, who as the judge, protector, and leader of all who lived on the manor was expected to defend the village and to administer the customary law. He enjoyed customary and hereditary rights, which tended in practice to be also rights to use in certain ways the lands of the manor and to monopolize certain activities requiring capital investments, such as the mills, presses, ovens, and workshops.

The common people of the village also were favored (and burdened) with certain customary rights and obligations. They were granted the right to cultivate fields for their own account, to use the pasture and wasteland, and to pass their holdings onto their heirs; they were bound, in return, to the manor and could not migrate or marry away from it without the lord's permission. They also owed the lord customary taxes upon death and marriage, and – that most essential link between the peasant or serf and the lord – they were obliged to perform specified labor services.

The main function of the lord, therefore, was to provide the public goods which each society must produce – protection and justice – while serfs or villeins in exchange provided labor, partly on their own holdings and partly on those of the lord. The proportion of time spent on each was predetermined, as we shall see later, by real economic factors and was carefully governed by the custom of the manor.

The classic manor by its very nature simply could not have been a stable economic organization but must have been constantly in a state of flux. When lords or peasants died, the ownership of the demesne or the rights to the tenant holdings were often split among the heirs. Gifts to the church and among the nobility also resulted in scattered claims to labor dues and to the produce of the manor's land. As these frequently fell by inheritance to outsiders, they were increasingly satisfied by payments in the form of a portion of the crop.

The manor, even at this time, was not an entirely closed or totally self-sufficient economic community. The fact that peasants often owed small payments to the lord in addition to labor dues implies a regular, if limited, participation in a market economy. During the ninth and tenth centuries small weekly markets appear to have proliferated. The uneven outputs of an agricultural economy gave a basis for mutually advantageous trade, and the provisioning of travelers allowed some exchange of food-stuffs and shelter for money. The lords themselves were occasional customers: the purchase of wood was common and the purchase of seed corn a regular affair. Apart from such strictly limited market transactions, the manor grew and produced much the greater part of the goods and services it consumed.

The lord of the typical manor did not exist entire to himself but held his place within a complex social structure specifying his relationship to other lords, and to the king, who was the ultimate source of his tenure. The Crown, responsible for the defense of the kingdom and needing resources to carry out that obligation, granted a specified area to the lord in return for equally clearly defined services. Thus feudalism was a fiscal system whereby the state obtained the resources to discharge its responsibilities to the kingdom.

The lords who held their land directly from the king were known as tenants *in capite*, or the chief tenants of the kingdom. Organizing their areas along the same lines, these chief tenants granted lands to others known as *mesne* tenants, who in turn further subdivided their holdings among others, identified as tenants *paravail*, whose duty was to make the land bear fruit. Only the king and the tenants *paravail* therefore occupied mutually exclusive positions: the king alone could never be a tenant, and the tenant *paravail* could never be a lord. Each of the intermediate parties was both tenant of the grantor and lord to his own grantees. Several persons thus had specified rights to the land that the tenant *paravail* actually worked.

Lands were granted by four distinct types of freeholding: tenure by knights' service, tenure in free and common socage, tenure in serjeanty, and tenure in frankalmoign. The fifth type of tenure (in which the majority of the population held their lands) was unfree and was called tenure in villeinage. Whereas a person holding land in free tenure could at any time return possession to his lord and depart, a villein was bound by law to remain on the land.

Tenure in knights' service granted use of land in return for the provision of a stipulated number of knights at the lord's command. Tenure in free and common socage was a grant of land in return for specified services such as money, produce, labor and attendance at the lords' court. Tenure by

28

serjeanty required in return certain military services, such as the provision of a given number of men in arms, transport, etc. that a modern quartermaster might provide. Tenure in frankalmoign was a grant to a man of the cloth whose duty was to provide religious services.

Let us examine a hypothetical case of the feudal organization in action. Suppose the king made a grant in knights' service to A in return for the promise of five knights to aid him. As the tenant *in capite*, A then granted lands to each of the five persons who were to serve him as knights. These in turn could make what grants they would. From his remaining portion of the original grant, Lord A would probably then grant a tract to X in free and common socage in return for an agreed annual amount of money, a certain number of bushels of grain, or similar good. Lord A would probably make grants to several individuals like X, since his economic well-being was mainly dependent upon the income derived from his holdings. Another portion Lord A might grant to Y, a clergyman, in frankalmoign as recompense for prayers offered for A, his relatives and ancestors. He might also grant some lands in serjeanty to Z, who would then be obliged to supply a certain number of attendants when A went to war. In some manner such as this Lord A would provide both for his own needs and for the discharging of his obligations to the Crown.

The lord of the manor we described above could have held his land in any of these ways. Since he directly possessed the land he was said to be seised in demesne; his lord (and the lords of his lord) clearly also held rights to the same land but were said to be seised in service, since they were not in direct possession. The land ultimately had to satisfy the tenurial obligations of both the lord in actual possession and those seised in service.

II

We have already seen that Western Europe at the beginning of the tenth century was mainly a vast wilderness. Between manors during the early Middle Ages little or no social or economic interactions occurred. The fundamental political institutions established during the Roman Empire had long since disappeared, replaced by feudalism. The high risk of traveling outside the manor made it far more efficient to adjust to economic needs by moving people when necessary, rather than by moving goods regularly; hence the individual settlements were fairly self-sufficient and isolated.

These conditions made the provision of public goods an important local matter. The ubiquitous piracy and brigandage, the less frequent but always possible incursions by Vikings, Huns or Moslems, made local defense a matter of prime concern. Individuals with superior military skills and equipment were urgently needed to protect the peasants who were unskilled in warfare and otherwise helpless. Here was the classic example of a public good, since it was impossible to protect one peasant family without also protecting their neighbors. In such cases coercion was necessary to overcome each peasant's incentive to let his neighbor pay the costs, and the military power of the lord provided the needed force. By virtue of that same force, the lord or seigneur was the logical person to settle disputes and in the last resort to enforce local law or customs; thus the provision of justice was added to his role of protector.

The lord's power to exploit his serfs, however, was not unlimited, but constrained (in the extreme case) by the serf's ability to steal away to seek illegal asylum on another manor. In the chaotic world of that period such runaways would probably not have been returned by the lord's neighboring rival. The abundance of land during the high Middle Ages made labor easily the most scarce, hence the most valuable, factor of production. Since the provision of public goods (protection and justice) is subject to economies of scale, over some range, some medieval lords were always in active competition with their peers to enlarge their estates, and each would have been vitally interested in the number of peasants inhabiting the village(s) of his manor, since the serfs produced the major portion of private goods for early medieval society. The larger the size of the village(s) the higher the lord's income would be. The village was organized on a communal basis, with its residents collectively tilling the open fields. This type of organization was economically rational: unprotected land at the time was almost as abundant as air and of no more economic value. Labor and capital, the scarce factors of production, alone set the boundaries for all output. Therefore the village would cultivate as much land as availability of the scarce factors would allow. Since it was found that resting a field in fallow for one year would allow the ground to retain its fertility, the village used twice as much arable land as was actually planted in any one year, the crops being rotated in a plan known as the two-field system.

While the land itself was of little economic value, its efficient use did require that it be tilled by a 'heavy' plow. The plow team including four to six oxen represented, for the time, an investment in physical capital prohibitively large for any single family to provide. Therefore the village entered into a co-operative arrangement, pooling their resources to make up a team. The individual peasant's share, initially determined by his contribution to the plow team, was designated in 'strips' – or the amount of land within the open field that could be plow-tilled in a day. These strips came to be accepted as the traditional or customary rights of the peasant, with his family entitled to enjoy the yearly produce of that particular plot. Whether by inheritance or, initially, to share the risk, peasant families typically came to hold strips within the open field and required a community decision about what and when to plant and harvest. Thus

30

communal agriculture developed as the typical method of producing staple crops, which were the bulk of private goods.

It still remains to be explained why the classic manor maintained a contractual relationship lord-and-tenant which took the form of labor obligations. The classic method of organizing the manor appears by today's standards a peculiar sharing arrangement. Certainly its counterpart would be hard to find in the modern world, but there lies the clue: the selection of labor obligations was determined by a condition generally absent today, namely, the restricted markets for produced goods.

Let us explore how this condition would affect the selection of a contractual arrangement. During and prior to the tenth century, the category of possible arrangements included: fixed wage payments in kind, fixed rents in kind, or an arrangement for sharing either inputs or outputs. The selection of a fixed wage payment in kind would have forced the lord to bear all the risks, plus the costs of management. The negotiation costs between the lord and the serf were apt to be high, since the lord would have had to supply the goods the peasant wished to consume or to negotiate in detail the rate of exchange for substitute payments. The costs of enforcement were also high, at least for the peasant, who would have had to sue in the manor court, dominated by the lord, to obtain redress for any contract violations.

Fixed rents in kind presented the opposite problem, that the peasant would have had to bear all the risk and management costs. Negotiation costs would still have been high, since the peasant needed to pay in rent the goods demanded by the lord. In the absence of a market for goods, either arrangement posed the problem of agreeing upon rates at which other goods might be substituted for those stipulated, and of negotiating the quality of goods to be delivered. Checking both the quantity and quality of the goods delivered for rents or wages would have also involved high enforcement costs and adjudication of the inevitable disputes was difficult and uncertain within the context of a legal system governed only by tradition.

A sharecropping arrangement, involving the sharing of either inputs or outputs, does spread the risk between parties according to their relative shares. The negotiation cost for sharing outputs is probably no different quantitatively or qualitatively in the absence of a product market than either a fixed or rent agreement. On the other hand, the negotiation cost for sharing *inputs* (i.e., labor dues) during and prior to the tenth century would have been lower than any of the other arrangements, especially since competition between lords for labor had resulted in a rudimentary market which established at least a range for the price of labor. As to the costs of enforcement; they are clearly higher in the case of sharing outputs than for either a fixed rent or a wage contract, since the size of crop must be determined as well as the quality. The enforcement cost for sharing inputs is probably the highest of any of the contractual forms considered, since on the manor this involved the sharing of labor, which always has an inclination to shirk. The historical literature is filled with references to this problem.

Against this background, the contractual arrangement of the classic manor can now be seen as an efficient arrangement for its day. The obligation of the serf to provide labor services to his lord and protector, an input-sharing arrangement, was chosen because given the constraint of high transaction costs involved in trading goods it was the most efficient. The almost total absence of a market for goods, plus the existence of a rudimentary market for labor, ensured that inputs could be shared with lower transaction costs than would be involved in other contractual arrangements. Competition between lords for labor restrained their natural bargaining power, allowing a customary value for labor to be determined outside a bilateral bargaining situation. The 'quaint' organization of the classic manor is therefore understandable as an appropriate response in the general absence of a market economy.

The same conditions responsible for manorialism also explain feudalism. The necessity was obvious to maintain a quasi-national or regional governmental defense against organized invasions and to adjudicate disputes between lords in those chaotic times. Once more, it was the absence of a market economy which determined the most efficient means of accomplishing this end, because without a market any alternative organization would have involved transaction costs which exceeded the benefits. Consider, for example, the maintenance of a standing or mercenary army, an obvious alternative. Lacking a market economy, only detailed and expensive negotiation could have specified the goods each soldier wanted in payment for his services.

Feudalism, in comparison, saved enough in negotiation costs to counter the high enforcement costs of such a decentralized political system. The granting by the king of large areas to be organized as petty kingdoms obviously provided the major lords, the tenants *in capite*, with a great deal of economic and political power. As protection against any potential threat by a coalition of lords, the king was well advised to remain a large landlord himself, so that he could field his own army to quell any rebellion. Nevertheless, as the history of medieval Europe relates, feudalism was inherently an unstable system, testifying to the innate high enforcement costs of the system. Only as long as the feudal world remained essentially a non-market economy did this classic form of political economy remain effectively in force. When the external conditions appropriate to both feudalism and manorialism changed, as we shall see in the next chapter, the natures of these two institutions were fundamentally altered.

5. THE HIGH MIDDLE AGES: A FRONTIER MOVEMENT

The Middle Ages from the tenth century onward brought striking changes to the economic and political environment of the Western World. Population expanded, regional and interregional commerce revived, new techniques were developed, and the classic institutions of both manorialism and feudalism changed beyond recognition.

I

A high rate of natural increase in population, although interrupted at times by wars, pillaging, and occasional famine or epidemic, was made possible by the abundance of virgin land. Sporadic waves of immigration supplemented the natural growth until the crowded manors spilled over into new arable lands on existing manors or surged outward to found entirely new manors on virgin lands in the wilderness. Sparse settlements in the frontier areas contrasted with dense agglomerations on the older sites. During the three centuries which began the second millennium A.D., this extension of the boundaries of settlement was destined to convert Western Europe from a vast wilderness into a well-colonized region.

Co-extensive with population growth, commerce began to push outward, spreading and blossoming along with the new settlements. Northern Europe set up brisk internal trade, which expanded with time to the classic lands of the Mediterranean. Southern Europe, with Venice in the lead, had begun before the tenth century to extend the limits and magnitude of trade throughout that region. Other Italian cities, notably Genoa and Pisa, quickly responded to the expanded commercial opportunities available, trading money, timber, iron and wood and metal products to the Moslems for spices, perfumes, ivory, fine textiles and oil. The traders of Southern Europe thus dealt mainly in items whose high value in relation to bulk led them to be classified by historians as luxury goods. From the tenth century the growing population of Northern Europe provided a limited but constantly expanding market for such goods, an opportunity quickly exploited by Italian merchants acting as middlemen.

Commerce within Northern Europe differed essentially from the trade between North and South. Items of a more basic character were exchanged in the North, where foodstuffs, especially grain, bulked large in the trade, and butter, cheese and fish were also staples. The wine trade grew in importance during these centuries, as did the exchange of timber and other forest products, like pitch, tar and furs. The main manufactured item entering this trade was cloth, more particularly woolens and linens.

Despite all the hazards presented by man and nature and the physical difficulties of moving merchandise in that day, the trade routes of Northern Europe were continually increasing in magnitude, complexity and geographical extent. Numerous fiscal extortions still hindered traders at frontiers and along the trade routes themselves, and merchants were forced by necessity to band together in caravans against the threat of piracy along the way. Travel by water was perhaps safer and because of its greater efficiency the preferred route, but it was not always available. Since travel by land or water was not only dangerous, but difficult and costly in time, men and equipment, the vast increase in commerce during this period occurred despite the burden of substantial transport costs.

The rise of trade within Northern Europe was accompanied by the establishment or revival of urban places. When Norsemen had been threatening Northern Europe, local nobles (dismayed by the lack of effective royal protection) had necessarily assumed responsibility for defending their own populations, often building local fortifications at strategic points. These places, along with the surviving Roman towns (partly because itinerant merchants naturally sought them out as safe stopping and resting places), became the cores around which the towns of the Middle Ages developed. Other steps followed in sequence. Local merchants set up shop to serve the needs of both the local area and the growing interregional trade; then artisans and craftsmen were attracted to these central places, until the settlements began to show the embryonic characteristics of what today we would recognize as urban areas. In the chronology of history, the growth of cities seems to have followed, with a lag, the expansion of population in a given area and to have been coincident with the establishment of interregional commerce.

The three centuries of the high Middle Ages, bursting out on new frontiers, creating a long-distance trade, busily establishing and expanding urban areas, were also productive of some new processes and technology. The powers of nature were being summoned to replace human and animal power, as water and wind began turning wheels to grind grain and to drive fulling mills. A new method of crop rotation, the three-field system, appeared and was gradually adopted in place of the traditional biennial rotation. It should be noted however that these changes, as spectacular as they appear, were still marginal additions, appendages to the manorial economy which dominated the economic organization of the era. They were spectacular because they were new, but in the scheme of things they are important more as portents of the future than for their initial impact upon economic organization.

Meanwhile the economic and political structure of medieval Europe was proving equally susceptible to the forces of change sweeping the Middle Ages. Increasingly both lords and serfs were attempting to obtain concessions from one another, to define legally the uses to which the manor's land and labor could be put, and to determine who was entitled to these privileges. Even the basic contractual arrangements between lord and serf were undergoing alteration, as the labor dues owed by the serf were more and more being commuted or transformed into annual money payments. The lord's demesne, at the same time, tended increasingly to be leased out in return for money rent payment. Thus by 1200 the classic manor of the tenth century had became an anachronism.

During the same period the traditional feudal contractual relationship between the king and his lords was undergoing a similar change. A money payment, called scutage, began to replace the specified traditional obligations. Tenure in knights' service and in serjeanty consequently became practically identical to free and common socage.

The researches of many historians have revealed the high Middle Ages as an era of change. By the dawn of the thirteenth century the political and economic structure of Western Europe had fundamentally changed from what it had been in the tenth century. In summary: population and commerce had expanded together; technological changes, if still limited in occurrence, had been widely adopted throughout the area; and the methods of agriculture had been adjusted to new conditions. And as a net result both manorialism and feudalism had undergone irreversible change.

II

The dynamic element that gave impetus to growth and development during the high Middle Ages was continued population growth. Even with current primitive technology, the relative abundance of land and other natural resources ensured a level of labor productivity above biological subsistence. The tendency for population to grow continued so long as additional virgin land could be brought into cultivation as the need arose, to feed additional mouths. This appears to have been the case in Western Europe until the thirteenth century.

However inexhaustible the lands of Northern Europe appear at this time to the historian, the land surrounding any given manor was inevitably limited in extent. Continued population growth eventually forced the people of the manor to take up land of inferior quality, having in the past already cleared the best virgin land available. When this occurred locally labor would have to be employed more intensively upon the existing arable land. This adjustment reflected the beginning of diminishing returns locally and thereafter additional units of labor employed actually reduced the marginal product of labor. The economic value of labor thus fell at the same time that land was becoming increasingly scarce and hence more valuable. These developments meant to the community that on a *per capita* basis the aggregate level of productivity was reduced. To the individual family, it meant that its young, if they remained in the area, were forced to delay marriage and the beginning of families. However, during the period in question suitable virgin lands still existed at the frontier. These young adults thus formed the pool of potential pioneers from which the colonists of the Middle Ages were drawn. By moving to the frontier these persons could obtain abundant land with which to work. Thus by migration they could escape the diminishing returns and falling incomes plaguing the manor of their birth. In this way population growth generated a frontier movement.

These local pockets of diminishing returns seem to have occurred first in France, sending settlers to the clay soils along the banks of the Saone and into the hills of Beaujolais, starting about 950. The draining of the marshes in Flanders, which required a substantial capital investment to reclaim the land, took place in about 1100. Evidence in the Domesday Book indicates that similar population growth occurred in England. During the centuries prior to the Norman invasion, colonization had brought settlement to all the major agricultural areas on the island.

The outsurge of population was changing the entire nature of the countryside. Once the space between manors had been virgin wilderness, its title usually vested in members of the high nobility who valued it chiefly as hunting preserves. Its human inhabitants, if any, had been of the sort celebrated in fairy tales – woodcutters, charcoal makers, iron-smelters, religious hermits, plus a liberal sprinkling of bandits. During this era, these wastes were being tamed, woods and pastures were shrinking back from villages, and fields were spreading in ever-expanding circles around the original settlements as adjacent areas were cleared during slack periods, used for a time as pasture and then, when well-drained, plowed for crops. As new fields were cultivated farther and farther from the village, some families tended to save travel time by moving out and enclosing small farms, until these family settlements filled spaces between adjacent manors and restricted their further expansion.

The actual colonization of wilderness areas required the co-operation of both lords and peasants, the latter to provide labor and the former to approve and protect the conversion of the wastelands and perhaps also to provide capital to finance the venture. The magnitude of effort and funds needed sometimes led to partnerships in which the lay lord provided the right to enclose the land and his associates the necessary funds and work-men. Because of their inherited wealth and their ability to communicate with peasants by way of parish churches, religious orders were often partners in such ventures.

Even while labor was losing value locally, it remained a precious com-modity on the frontier. Would-be founders of new manors had to seek out peasants aggressively, even to the point of limiting their own powers by offering grants and privileges to entice potential emigrants. Often they would require no labor dues at the beginning but only specified levies in kind, and sometimes the revenues from the lord's traditional privileges and monopolies were initially the sole source of revenue to the ambitious *entrepreneur* of a new manor. Peasants who succumbed to the lure of the frontier could either purchase their freedom from their lord, have it purchased for them by the lord organizing a new manor, or steal away in the night. It is clear that large numbers of them followed one or another of these paths to the frontier.

The wilds of Western Europe were gradually settled in this manner. New villages flourished, and their success in raising revenues for the enterprising nobility encouraged further attempts to promote colonization. The frontier provided a serf with an alternative living, a fact that all lords had to take into account or risk losing their serfs to the colonies. Thus competition between lords for laborers placed real limits on the exploitation of manorial peasants. The alternative of moving to the frontier was probably more important in limiting peasant exploitation than the presence of growing towns.

The frontier movement which created differing population densities (man/land ratios) throughout Western Europe also resulted, as economics would predict, in creating gains from specialization and trade. As noted earlier, the gains from trade were also stimulated as the moving frontier settled areas with different natural resources. The wine areas of France, for example, provided a whole new basis for trade. Since each region would concentrate upon its comparative advantage, areas of high population density could produce more efficiently labor-intensive goods, trading them for land-intensive goods from regions less densely settled. The expansion of the cloth industry during the Middle Ages is a good example. Major centers of production sprang up in Flanders, Picardy, Bruges, Languedoc, Lombardy and other areas of relatively dense habitation specializing in labor-intensive manufacture. Flanders, for example, during the high Middle Ages became dependent on trade to furnish its population with the most basic foodstuffs, exchanging cloth for cereals and wine. Cloth manu-facturing also provided a valuable commodity to exchange for the luxury products of the East.

Local trade also prospered with the settling of spaces between manors.

An increase in local population density widened the market, lowering transactions costs and initially encouraging the establishment of such industries as handicrafts and various services. The manor now had an alternative to basic self-sufficiency, namely the potential gains from specialization and trade.

III

The development and extension of a market for goods altered the basic economic conditions to which the institution of the manor had been the efficient response. If contracting parties now chose to set up an arrangement for fixed rent, fixed wage or the sharing of output, it was no longer necessary to specify the consumption bundle in detail, because any of these remittances, whether received in money or in kind, could be exchanged at reasonable cost for the desired goods. A market, even as limited as the one under consideration, lowered the pure transactions cost of any of these contracts relative to the traditional labor-sharing arrangement.

The confrontation between 'changing times' and 'changing customs' was never more literally enacted than in the alteration of manorial contractual forms after the inception of the market economy. 'Customs of the manor' had set time-honored precedents for fulfilling contractual obligations as well as for all other aspects of manorial life – from the nature of the crops to be sown to the times at which various functions were performed. As these customs were now brought under the pressure of altering economic conditions, the basic contractual arrangement between lord and peasant began slowly to shift away from labor dues toward one of the other contractual forms.

The change was taking place, however, within the old fundamental institutional setting which had evolved to deal satisfactorily with a slowly changing self-sufficient manor. It is not surprising that the customs of the manor yielded only very slowly in most cases. It was hard to change what had been sanctified by tradition and was the only impersonal law of the land. Moreover, even when change would have been an immediate advantage to the peasants they were inclined to cling to the anchoring force of custom, which had been a real protection to them in the past in dealing with overzealous lords. When the passive resistance of a united peasantry had been bolstered by 'custom', they had held a strong position indeed. During the initial centuries of the high Middle Ages, the customs were carried in men's minds, and oral recitation defined the very law by which the manor was governed. Because during the Middle Ages economic conditions changed only slowly, manorial customs had been altered only by the gradual modification of specific conditions. While over the centuries the sum of these minor changes may have amounted to fundamental alteration, during a peasant's lifetime the law appeared fixed. Now, with new economic conditions, the costs of negotiating efficient changes in the nature of the contract were vastly increased by the solemn weight of opposed patriarchal custom. It was easier, and far cheaper in negotiation costs, to move forward by slow steps that could be viewed as minor variations of past practices rather than as clear innovations.

Economic historians long held to the almost classic theory that the decline of the manor was precipitated exactly, as we contend here, by the rise of a market economy. That explanation has fallen into disrepute. But in the context of our argument, the presence of a market for goods is clearly sufficient to explain the eventual disappearance of the essential element of the manorial system: the sharing of inputs in the form of labor dues. To recapitulate: the labor obligation was for its time an efficient form of contract because any alternative arrangement involved (in the absence of a market for goods) the necessity to specify a consumption bundle and to enforce the quantity and quality agreed upon. The traditional manorial contract, however, suffered high enforcement costs because the labor had to be supervised and policed against shirking. *Ceteris paribus*, free labor, which is voluntarily given, is more productive than that of serfs which is not. When the development of a market removed the need to specify the consumption bundle, allowing instead payments in money or kind, the balance of efficiency tilted toward other contractual forms with lower enforcement costs.

Obviously, then, as the market for goods widened and became more efficient, some form of contractual arrangement other than labor dues would eventually appear, although the exact time and form of the transition would depend on prior conditions on the manor. One contractual form that emerged during the twelfth century, if not earlier, was of the following general type. Lords increasingly, at their discretion, annually commuted the labor dues owed them for a fixed money payment which came to be accepted as the customary price. They also tended to lease out portions of their demesne for a fixed rent payment. In some places, such as the vineyards of France, a share cropping arrangement developed. Lords whose manors were not on the frontier had an additional incentive, in the absence of inflation, to choose money payments at the customary level in lieu of labor, since diminishing returns to a growing manorial population were reducing the real value of labor. The money payment, fixed by custom, soon ceased to reflect the true value of labor as diminishing returns continued in densely settled areas during the course of the twelfth century. Thus the lord gained by annually electing to commute as the value of the peasants' services declined; at the same time, however, this may have been offset by the fact that the customary fixed rent on land also failed to reflect the rising real value of land, acting much as rent controls do today. To renegotiate the rent periodically would have been a prohibitively expensive task under existing customs, so the lord of the land often circumvented the 'control' by calling on a prior customary device known as the succession duty or entry fine. Similar to modern 'key money' in its original form, the entry fine, which had to be negotiated only when a new tenant took up the land, came to serve a new function by reflecting the increased value of the land over its customary annual rent. Thus, it exemplified the slow process of change within the framework of existing custom as a means of adjusting to a disequilibrium – in this case, the increase in the value of land relative to labor.

The frontier movement that began in the tenth century and continued through the twelfth created, as we have seen, widely differing conditions within the regions that composed the feudal economy. The market for commodities was greater in more densely settled areas than on the frontier, but so too was the weight of custom. We might well expect what actually occurred – a great diversity in manorial organization – but the trend was clear: money payments were replacing labor dues.

The economic relationship between lords (feudalism) was also altered by the rise of a market economy. Where previously the payment of a standing army could only have been arranged by difficult and expensive negotiations and perhaps by equally high costs in delivering or adjusting the compensation, a single money payment would now suffice. The creation of a market economy by significantly reducing transactions costs allowed public goods (as well as private goods) to be produced more efficiently than before.

Where previously noble tenants had personally performed services or provided goods, they could now instead pay a money fine. Tenants in knights' service tended to substitute for each promised knight a sum of money (often 2 marks, or £1, in England) representing a knight's remuneration at 6 pence a day for the annual due of forty days. The price of a knight's commutation came to be fixed at this rate. The annual obligation of tenants in chief went for a higher price, negotiated directly with the king and also designated as fines.

The commutation of feudal dues for a money payment similar to today's tax payment was advantageous to both tenants and lords. Lords received the means to produce public goods independently of the personal services of their tenants; tenants were freed to specialize in administration and production. This event was of some historical importance. Kings and major lords were now able to employ a standing or mercenary army which could be used at will. These lords were also freed from the forty-day limit on armed service and could raise armies when and where they wished and as large as they could afford. This development, which becomes a major factor from the thirteenth century on, set off a political scramble for revenues which ultimately influenced both the rise of nation-states and the paths of economic growth within Europe.

IV

Because agriculture during the Middle Ages almost completely dominated economic life, with probably more than 90 percent of the population living directly off the land, changes in land use are of paramount importance for this study. Shortly before the beginning of the ninth century a new system of agricultural organization – the three-field system – was inaugurated in parts of Western Europe. Its introduction and slow diffusion to replace the traditional two-field planting has been considered a major technological advance, bringing about a significant improvement in productivity.

Under the two-field system all arable land had been plowed but only one half of it planted to crops, the other half being left in fallow to recuperate its fertility. The second year, the fallow field was planted and the recently harvested field left barren. The three-field system now divided the arable land of the manor into three parts. In the archetype, one field was plowed and planted to wheat during the autumn, the second plowed and planted in the spring to oats, barley or legumes, such as peas or beans, and the third field was plowed and left to fallow. The next year crops were rotated, the first field being left to fallow, the second planted to winter crops, the third to spring crops. The third year the first field bore spring crops, the second was in fallow, and the third in winter wheat. The fourth year began another cycle.

Historians have cited manifold advantages of the three-field system. The arable land bearing crops was increased by 50 percent. Agricultural labor was spread more evenly throughout the year, as plowing, planting, and harvesting times were staggered between seasons as well as fields. The two harvest periods reduced the chance of famine due to season crop failures. The increased output of oats allowed peasants to replace the ox with the more efficient horse. The legume crops provided a useful vegetable protein as a dietary supplement to the usual breadstuffs. The now well-known nitrogen-fixing properties of legumes maintained the fertility of the soil, countering the effect of smaller fallow areas under the three-field system.

In view of all these advantages, historians have been hard pressed to explain the slow rate of diffusion of this allegedly superior technique. Although its rate of acceptance has not been fully studied, we know that this system originated in the late eighth century in the area between the Seine and the Rhine, in the land of the Franks, and that its spread from there throughout Western Europe took several centuries. Not until the twelfth century was triannual rotation even introduced into England.

How do we account for such slow adoption? When historians have considered this problem at all, they have stressed climatic limitations, the common resistance of peasants to change, and the cost of obtaining consensus when this involved rearranging the ownership of strips. Thus, implicitly, the explanation for the slow rate of diffusion lies in a cost–benefit decision: the psychological and transaction costs of instituting the three-field system counterbalanced the significant benefits it promised. Conservative peasants would watch and wait and observe results before committing their fields to a new method.

To continue this cost–benefit approach more explicitly, let us first examine the benefits of the three-field system in the light of economic principles. That the arable land under cultivation was increased and that labor was spread more evenly throughout the year offered real improvements, because the increasing scarcity of land relative to labor had created an incentive to use agricultural lands more intensively (that is, to use more labor per unit of land). Even during the ninth century, when settlements were generally sparse in Western Europe, certain local villages were densely populated, as witnessed by the rise of assarting, and finally of colonization. But as population continued to increase in some areas, diminishing returns to labor would reduce its value still further relative to that of land, making it profitable, indeed necessary, to use more labor per unit of land. It is interesting that the practice of double-plowing the fallow, a clear application of more labor per unit of land, was not generally adopted until the twelfth century, when labor was in even more abundant supply.

Other virtues of the three-field system would also be enhanced by the twin facts of a growing population and the local onset of diminishing returns. The assarting of new fields meant, in time, the total disappearance of wilderness areas having any potential for cultivation. Limited, now, were the woodlands where a hungry peasant might go hunting, gather wild food, or mast-feed swine. Vegetable protein had to substitute for the missing pork and wild game. In economic terms, animal protein had become more expensive than vegetable protein, because the raising of animals was more land-intensive and land had become an increasingly scarce factor of production. The reduction of the natural wastelands also supposedly led the horse into harness where once oxen had strained at their yokes. The horse is reputed to be from 50 to 90 percent more biologically efficient as a source of energy; however if the ox (a natural 'grass burner') can be fed off wasteland at virtually no expense, while the horse must be fed relatively expensive oats, then the ox is economically the more efficient of the two. But if either animal must be fed similar amounts of grain and/or hay (now relatively expensive) the horse would be the logical choice.

It is clear therefore that the three-field system became an improved form of organization only when a growing population led to diminishing returns to labor, because then scarce land had to be conserved and used more intensively. In earlier epochs, when land was abundant on every hand, the classic two-field system with its extravagant use of waste had fully met the requirements of economic efficiency.[1]

The discovery that the three-field system is an economically rational response to a changing land–labor ratio helps explain its relatively slow diffusion throughout Western Europe. Only when land became scarce could the net benefits of the three-field system outweigh the benefits of the two-field system. The three-field system should therefore be expected to follow, with a lag, an increase in the density of population across Western Europe. It is probably no accident that the new method was not introduced in England until the twelfth century, only shortly before diminishing returns became a general condition throughout the country and certainly well after they had become a grim fact of life in localities where the three-field system was first accepted.

Viewed in this way, the three-field system cannot be considered a major improvement in efficiency, but merely a reaction to a changed situation. Clearly, communities that experienced diminishing returns and did not adopt the three-field system were worse off then they could have been. But it is also obvious that output per man was higher in those areas where land was still as abundant as air and the two-field system was appropriate, than it was in other localities where land was scarce, diminishing returns to labor existed and the three-field system proved more efficient.

V

We have examined how the widening of the market led to urban settlement, specialization, and trade. The same phenomenon also affected the state of medieval technology. The expanding local markets for grain and the regional and interregional markets for woolens led to the adoption and spread of water-powered mills for grinding grain and fulling cloth. It is noteworthy that most of the significant technological advances were adoptions and adaptations of inventions made outside Western Europe. For reasons already hinted at and to be developed later, the institutional environment of medieval Europe did not encourage the process of invention.

The widening of local markets after the year 1000 did, however,

---

[1] If the three-field system had been a clear gain in efficiency it would have been adopted quickly on the frontier as new manors were cleared and settled. It would have thus spread from the eighth century with settlement until by 1200 it would have been the dominant form of agriculture organization. It was not; the reason was that the three-field system was efficient only when the price of labor had fallen relative to that of land. The three-field system was an adjustment to a change in relative factor prices, rather than a technological change.

encourage the dissemination of known technological achievements such as water mills and windmills. Such capital improvements, harnessing natural power, represented large potential gains in efficiency, but they required capital – often a great deal of capital for that day. Therefore they were economical only when used to produce what to previous generations of Northern Europeans would have appeared to be immense volumes of goods. Only notable increases in local population density and the expansion of interregional trade could justify production on such a scale. Since the same increase in densities eventually brought locally diminishing returns to labor and a consequent rise in local land values, which made the feeding of animals more costly than before, a further incentive was created to harness the forces of nature to replace draft animals.

By the eleventh century, water-driven mills had become an everyday sight. The Domesday Book in 1086 recorded 5624 mills for 3000 communities, and there is no reason to believe that England was technologically in advance of the Continent. In addition to grinding grain, water power was being harnessed to more and wider activities, driving saws (probably a tenth-century development), operating fulling mills and powering the triphammers of forges.

The institutional setting of the high Middle Ages certainly did not encourage research on a socially appropriate scale. Yet technological improvements were not totally lacking because the expanding market, bringing specialization in its wake, offered somewhat greater private rewards to an individual who could improve methods of production. The expanding local market allowed some capital goods with high fixed costs to be employed efficiently for the first time. At the same time, the trend toward specialization was concentrating men's natural inventive curiosity on more limited problems and thus lowering the costs of discovery.

Experiments with water power during this period also included some attempts to build tidal mills. Much more importantly, the power of the wind was successfully harnessed, and this does appear to have been a Western triumph, inspired as the movement of populations took them away from the sources of water power. Wind, they discovered, while less reliable than a flowing stream, was more widely available and not subject to freezing. The water-turned wheel found a logical extension in the great windmills that soon dotted the plains of Northern Europe – a common feature of the landscape by the beginning of the thirteenth century.

While new sources of power were being tapped, attempts were made to improve techniques for the increasing volume of commercial goods. New mechanisms for the transmission of power included the pulling force of bent saplings to drive bellows and to turn lathes, and a treadle, also used to turn lathes and power weaving looms, was introduced.

These gradual developments in the purely economic sphere (which in retrospect appear substantial) can all be accounted for by the extension of the market. The institutional environment discouraged any more, since no inventor or *entrepreneur* could be sure of gaining all or any substantial part of the benefits from his efforts. Secrecy was the only recourse against copying by all hands. Research and development under these constraints could not take place on anything approaching the socially optimal scale.

The one exception to this rule was in the development of weaponry. In an age of incipient warfare, the political return to the development of a new weapons system or the improvement of existing systems could be very great, and the high nobility of the period were openhanded in supporting research in this area. A few spin-offs to peacetime uses resulted.

In summary then, technology did move forward during the Middle Ages, though its progress was hampered and chilled by an inhospitable climate. There was no institutional assurance that the private rate of return to inventors would equal the social rate, yet in the absence of such guarantees the very size of expanding local and regional markets served to raise the private rate of return above that which had existed during the Carolingian period. This especially encouraged the dissemination of already existing techniques. The unstable political system supported some research in fields appropriate to warfare, which inevitably had spin-offs appropriate to the economic sector. In general, however, the fact that any new developments could freely be copied, without compensation, served to discourage the investment of resources in any research or development beyond that naturally attributable to specialization. Since secrecy was the only recourse of the inventor, dissemination of the benefits of the new development to society was blocked, thus reducing or delaying that increase in productivity which constitutes economic growth.

What can be said, then, to sum up the performance of the economy of Western Europe during most of the high Middle Ages? Certainly extensive growth continued apace, creating a market system where none had effectively existed. This development allowed reduction in transaction costs and specialization of functions, and stimulated the widespread adoption of new sources of power. Each of these phenomena could in turn have tended to increase *per capita* incomes, raising productivity. Countering these improvements, overpopulation and local diminishing returns reduced productivity in agriculture, but this effect was at least partially offset by the frontier movement and the limited adoption of the three-field system.

6. THIRTEENTH-CENTURY EUROPE

The thirteenth century was not like other centuries. First of all, it was not of a hundred years' duration. We do not know when it began nor for certain when it ended, so we cannot know how long it was. The reason for this innocence lies in the fact that for economic historians the thirteenth century refers to the temporal duration of a unique set of forces and is much more easily described than dated.

The thirteenth century brought the end of the frontier movement in Western Europe, but it did not bring the end of population growth, which continued at an impressive rate. Urban places expanded. Trade and commerce flourished locally, regionally and internationally. In short, this was a dynamic era; the culmination of an expansion that had begun in the tenth century. During its indeterminant span of years this era links the growth of a frontier society, where everyone seems to have gained with the horrors of the 'hateful' fourteenth century where everyone lost. This bridge between two such diverse periods of medieval history was opulent, filled with contrasts, paradoxes and interesting historical questions. The thirteenth century represents the autumn of the Middle Ages. The paramount questions: Why did the extensive and intensive growth apparent in previous centuries not continue? Why could the economies of Western Europe not escape at this time the Malthusian specter that had previously haunted mankind? These are the important questions and we shall attempt to answer them in this chapter.

I

Quantitative information for any period before 1300 is sparse and this limits the accuracy with which we can draw detailed inferences about the evolution of the economy. Although the general contours are clear, any precise dating of the changes must remain speculative. On the other hand, the qualitative information is abundant. The thirteenth century was evidently an era of substantial expansion, a period of real economic awakening in Europe, a time of relative and absolute price changes, and of expanding trade and commerce. All of this is documented in contemporary descriptions and accounts.

Every economic historian who has studied this period agrees also that population was growing in Western Europe, probably more rapidly at the peripheries than at the centers of settlement, where diminishing returns to additional laborers had already been encountered. Therefore, we suppose that England and Germany probably experienced higher population growth rates than other areas. It has been estimated that the population of England increased almost 250 percent between Domesday (1086) and the year 1300. While estimates of this type are obviously subject to large errors, local studies also seem to indicate an increase of roughly this magnitude.

The differences in population densities between regions present some striking contrasts. Southern Europe, particularly Northern Italy, was by far the most densely populated. The territory of Florence may have contained as many as 200 inhabitants per square mile. In the era just before the Black Death, the kingdom of Naples may have possessed about 3.3 million inhabitants, or approximately 100 inhabitants per square mile, roughly equalling the density of France, with a total estimated population of 16 to 17 million inhabitants. Catalonia, on the outskirts of Europe's population movement, had perhaps 43 inhabitants per square mile. The great cities of Milan and Venice each boasted a population of perhaps 200,000, and other Italian urban centers, such as Florence, Genoa, Naples, and Palermo, may have contained as many as 100,000. The giants of their times, these cities far exceeded in size their nearest rivals.

Outside Italy, Barcelona had approximately 40,000 inhabitants, and Paris probably could not count 100,000 persons within its environs. The area of Western Europe that reached the greatest urban–commercial development during the thirteenth century, however, was the Netherlands. Strategically located at the natural crossroads of the expanding commerce of Western Europe, they became the locus for centers of manufacturing and commerce. In the Meuse River Valley a number of towns engaged in the metal industry, and those in the Valley of the Scheldt concentrated on woolen textiles and commerce. Bruges became the leading port of Northern Europe during the century, and neighboring towns flourished in the wake of its prosperity. Ghent and Bruges, at their height, reached possibly 50,000 inhabitants each. The extraordinary feature, however, was less the absolute size of individual towns than the general metropolitan nature of this area, where the urban population at this early date probably exceeded the rural, a phenomenon unique outside the Italian peninsula. England remained relatively unurbanized during the period, although London, its largest city, approximately doubled in size from about 20,000 to 40,000 persons. Since both the total European population and the population of cities increased, it is impossible to state whether Europe became more urbanized over the century.

An examination of the price history of the thirteenth century cannot be as conclusive as we would like, because of the paucity of data covering the entire calendar century. We do have several series of agricultural prices which span the whole period, but non-agricultural prices and wages are roughly continuous only for the last half of the century, with only scattered entries for years prior to 1250. Only a general impression of the trend in rents can be obtained from the surviving scanty observations.

Nevertheless, an aggregate picture of the changes in relative prices can be constructed. It is clear that in England the price of wheat rose substantially, increasing, in terms of silver, from 140 in 1180–99 (where the period 1160–99 is the base of 100) to 325 in 1300–19.[1] Other series, expressed in units of current account, corroborate the general rise in the price of wheat and other agricultural products. The accepted view is that agricultural prices rose more than the prices of non-agricultural goods and also more rapidly than wages. In a recent review of the English economy of the Middle Ages, M. M. Postan provides some evidence of sharply rising rents in the late thirteenth century. He describes a drastic shift from pasture to arable land, a decline in yields, and an end to colonization because the last land reserves were being exhausted.[2] A resultant rise in agricultural prices while money wages remained stable suggests to him that real wages fell by 25 percent between 1208 and 1225, and by another 25 percent between 1225 and 1348.

The following pattern emerges: agricultural prices rose relative to most non-agricultural prices and also to money wages, but perhaps not so much as did rents. While evidence for the rest of Europe is even less complete than the meager information about England, it appears to confirm the same trends.

One question remains. Did the general price level rise during the thirteenth century at nearly the same rate as did one of its major components, agricultural prices? It was the opinion of such historians as Pirenne and Bloch that it did. Recent work on the English economy seemingly agrees. A simple exercise in logic suggests that the views stated above are probably correct. Ask the following question: given our inadequate information about non-agricultural prices, how much would these have had to fall to keep the general price level constant and still allow for the known increases in agricultural prices? The information on wheat prices presented above showed an increase during the century of about 230 percent. Bearing in

[1] D. L. Farmer, 'Grain Price Movements in 13th Century England', *Economic History Review*, 2nd series, 10 (1957–8), 207 *seq.*

[2] 'The Agrarian Life of the Middle Ages', *Cambridge Economic History*, 2nd ed., vol. 1 (Cambridge University Press, 1966), pp. 552–9.

mind that agricultural products probably accounted for over 80 percent of all goods produced in England, the price of non-agricultural goods would have had to fall over 90 percent to keep the aggregate price level constant. Such a phenomenon would certainly have been noted as one of the major economic events of the century. It is logical to conclude that the thirteenth century witnessed a general inflation as well as a dramatic change in relative prices and a substantial decline in real wages. This was probably true for Western Europe in general as well as for England.

If quantitative data on population and prices are sparse, data on the volume of international trade are even more limited and scattered. Here we must rely on abundant qualitative descriptions to give us some idea of the great expansion in trade, both internal and international, which occurred during the Middle Ages, reaching its culmination in the thirteenth century. The leaders in this growing commerce, the great seaport cities of Italy, were joined by some inland cities like Florence and many other smaller centers of internal trade to become part of the expanding international network. In addition there were lesser cities scattered around the rim of the Mediterranean basin. Venice continued as pacesetter throughout the century. Venice's expansion was closely followed by Genoa, Pisa, Amalfi and Palermo. These cities through exchange and trade linked together such far-flung places as Constantinople on the borders of Asia, areas along the north coast of Africa and such Southern European cities as Marseilles and Barcelona. The Mediterranean became a gigantic highway for Italian merchant vessels.

Nor was the trade network of medieval Europe confined to the Mediterranean. First Genovese and then Venetian ships ventured to Northern Spain, then England, and finally to the Netherlands. The Italian expansion was not confined to the sea; their merchants also ventured overland into Germany and to the fairs of the Champagne district of France. Thus, during the thirteenth century, the famous ages-old Mediterranean commerce was connected by both land and sea to the growing trade of Northern Europe. By the end of the thirteenth century Italian merchants were residing in all the Northern European areas.

The trade of Northern Europe was of a different character. Except for furs, it was essentially a trade in bulkier, low-value commodities. Here too, grain was a major item in international trade. Surplus-producing areas such as the Baltic region, England in earlier decades and some of the areas of France exported grain to the more densely populated, deficit-food areas of Flanders and the Low Countries in general.

A major trade of Northern Europe was in wine. Increasingly during the century qualitative differences in environment led to a number of differentiated major wine-making centers. Poitou, Gascony, the center of the great Bordeaux wines, Burgundy and Moselle were, even at this time, great centers for the production of specialized quality wines. The wine trade, during this century, became a major employer of shipping throughout Europe (particularly from Gascony to England).

Another major trade was lumber, used in shipbuilding and in crating and packaging as well as for a wide variety of construction purposes. Deficit lumber areas, such as Flanders, received large-scale shipments from the still densely wooded forests of Northern Europe.

The wool-cloth trade was probably the most valuable in Northern Europe. The supply of raw wool came primarily from England, and the geographical center for its manufacture developed in Flanders, where the neighboring towns of Bruges, Ypres, Ghent and Douai became the great cloth centers of Northern Europe. The cloth trade probably accounted for Bruges' growth into the most important market west of the Alps. Merchants from all over Northern Europe brought their goods there to exchange them for cloth or the produce of other areas. The easy access to the Low Countries by water, coupled with its central geographic position, ensured the importance of this area in the growth of the commerce of Northern Europe. The decline of the Champagne Fairs and the opening of a sea route to the Mediterranean combined to ensure the pre-eminence of Bruges as a commercial center by the end of the thirteenth century.

As long-distance commerce developed, local markets kept pace, expanding and flourishing all over Northern Europe. In England, for example, during the first seventy-five years of the century over 2200 separate charters for markets and fairs were granted by the Crown and it is safe to assume that other areas experienced similar commercial developments.

Without quantitative data there is no way of providing a precise estimate of the growth of commerce or of the *per capita* value of trade over time. Yet contemporary descriptions of thirteenth-century Europe leave no doubt that at all levels – local, regional and international – commercial activity was burgeoning, self-sufficiency was on the decline, and specialization was being practiced on a scale hitherto unknown to Western Europe. A true market economy was taking form, but within a context where the total economy remained overwhelmingly agricultural, and where farm and primary products still probably accounted for the vast bulk of goods traded within Northern Europe.

II

The bits and pieces of historical evidence presented above can, with the aid of economic theory, be made to reveal a theoretically consistent picture. The pattern of relative prices during the century, as sketched above, was influenced by changes in relative productivity between the economic sectors of the economy and/or between the factors of production. The factors that influence productivity are such things as technological change, changes in organization, and differential rates of expansion between the factors of production. Clearly it was the latter, specifically the rapid growth of population relative to the fixed supply of land, that accounted for the pattern of Western European economic growth during the thirteenth century.

Population had been continually growing throughout Western Europe since the tenth century. Sometime prior to the beginning of the thirteenth century, however, additions to the labor force in most areas encountered general diminishing returns. As we have seen, the disappearance of the frontier dictated that thereafter further additions to the labor force be applied more intensively to land already in cultivation. As population continued to grow throughout the century, the marginal productivity of labor further declined; hence wages fell relative to the value of land.

The prices of agricultural goods, produced under conditions of diminishing returns, now increased in relation to the prices of non-agricultural goods not so burdened. Arable land had become fixed relative to the growing labor force; but since labor employed in non-agricultural pursuits (where land played an inconsequential role in the production process) was not so affected, non-agricultural output could still increase in response to increased demand at constant cost. The rise in total output of Western Europe during the thirteenth century therefore necessarily involved higher prices for agricultural goods relative to other products.

The general presence of diminishing returns in the agricultural sector was bad news for a growing population, the vast majority of whom were still engaged on the land. A *per capita* decline in productivity in the dominant sector of the economy simply meant less output, *ceteris paribus*, for each person engaged in agrarian pursuits. Furthermore, the more abundant crops needed to feed a growing population demanded a redistribution of income between the two major factors of production – land and labor. Throughout the century the rewards to labor declined while land brought ever greater returns to its owners. The bulk of the population, as a direct result, suffered a sharp decline in economic welfare. As an indirect result, significant strains began to tug at the existing agrarian institutional arrangements.

Meanwhile, however, as population growth was pressing directly downward on the standard of living, it was expanding the possibilities for trade. While this secondary effect tended to reinforce the changes in relative prices, it operated in the opposite direction on the level of well-being because it led to improvements in aggregate productivity.

As we have seen, the growth of population in Western Europe, by accenting the differences in factor endowments between regions, had created a foundation for the enormously expanded trade, stimulating specialization in production, extending the basis for commerce, reducing transaction costs and encouraging more use of the market mechanism to exploit specialized resource endowments. Productivity obviously benefited from specialization, from the division of labor, and from the greater efficiency in techniques, organization, and institutions which appeared during the century in almost every sector of the economy. Even in agriculture, had it not been subject to such severe diminishing returns, productivity gains overall would have resulted from increased production for the market.

Improvements in productivity were probably greater in the Italian cities than in Northern Europe. Their ability to support the described population densities suggests an efficiency in economic organization well surpassing that exhibited by Northern Europe during the Middle Ages. The extension of international specialization and division of labor coupled with Italian leadership in the innovation of productive institutional arrangements, discussed below, allowed those areas to capture the gains from trade. Their ability to reap the benefits from an extensive commerce is the underlying factor in the precocious development of the Italian cities.

The growth of population itself therefore tended to widen the market, making it feasible to introduce new production techniques, organizations and institutions. Such changes as these, both increasing the productivity of the manufacturing sector and reducing the cost of using the market to exchange products, would reinforce the shifts in relative prices that occurred during the century.[3] However, the increased productivity also raised incomes and the level of welfare, tending to offset somewhat the direct effects of diminishing returns in the agricultural sector. Any improvements that occurred in the agricultural sector would, of course, work against the actually observed changes in relative prices and in favor of raising the level of welfare. We shall argue below that due to the existing institutional arrangements in agriculture any improvements in this sector would have had only a minor influence on *per capita* incomes.

It is certain that during the thirteenth century the beneficial secondary

[3] The costs of transactions divide the agricultural sector and the manufacturing sector from each other and from the final consumer. These costs can be viewed in the same way as a tax. As the costs are reduced the prices to the consumer and the producer and the output of each sector are affected according to the elasticities of supply and demand. Supply in manufacturing can be assumed to be perfectly elastic and in agriculture to show some positive elasticity. Thus a general decline in transaction costs would not influence the price received by the manufacturer, but would reduce by the full amount the price paid by the consumer. In agriculture, both the consumer and producer would share, according to the relevant elasticities. Thus the price paid by the consumer would not fall by the full amount. Industrial prices paid by the consumer would thus fall relative to the prices paid by the consumer for agricultural goods. Thus the terms of trade between the two sectors would move in exactly the same direction as the movement caused by diminishing returns in agriculture. The welfare consequences are quite different between the two causes of a shift in the terms of trade.

effects of population growth on overall productivity proved inadequate to counter its adverse primary effects. The need to feed greater and greater numbers of mouths simply swamped the resulting improvements in productivity. While the rise of a market economy could mitigate local famines, it was to prove powerless to avert more general disasters.

Localized famines, widespread before 1200, loomed less threateningly during the thirteenth century. Produce from areas of surplus was for the first time available to feed other sections suffering bad harvests. Certainly this was a clear gain, yet as population grew over wider areas so did the specter of diminishing returns. Even more widespread was the decline in *per capita* income, especially for poorer groups. Historically, the plague of 1347–51 has been designated as the point of demise of this century of expansion; actually a more probable turning point was the calendar end of the thirteenth century, which brought the advent of general famines.

In the decade 1307–17 famine spread throughout Europe and foreshadowed a more general crisis – although it remained for the pestilence to stamp a final exclamation point at the end of an era.

III

The basic economic relationships that developed during the thirteenth century have now become clear, but at best they only partially explain why the economy did not achieve self-sustaining growth during this period. The answer lies in the nature of the economic organizations and institutions that developed in response to the driving economic forces disclosed and explained above.

The consequences of expanding trade for the agricultural and institutional structure of the non-agricultural sector were dramatic. During the late twelfth and all of the thirteenth century, experimentation was undertaken to develop secondary institutional arrangements designed to capture the potential profits inherent in the commercial sector. These were the profits that would stem from reducing information costs, spreading risks, and internalizing externalities. As one would expect, the initial leadership in these institutional changes came from Southern Europe, particularly from the Italian cities, which having long dominated the trade of the Mediterranean enjoyed the most extensive market.[4]

In order to pursue overseas trade merchants from these cities devised contractual arrangements known as the *commenda* and the *societas*. Both involved co-operation between a traveling partner, called *tractator*, and an investing partner who stayed on land – called *stans*. These contractual

---

[4] Invention and innovation are encouraged by the extension of the market, for the reasons given in the preceding chapter. It must be noted again that because the inventor cannot capture all the gains from his research, less than the socially optimal amount will be undertaken.

forms for a single voyage were designed to provide capital and a working partner by a voluntary association, to spread and reduce risks, and to improve information flows.[5] The *commenda* and the *societas* thus improved access to profitable foreign ventures.

Another secondary institutional arrangement developed in this period was deposit banking. Banks of deposit were not a new institution, having probably existed in Roman times, but their revival dates from the end of the twelfth and the beginning of the thirteenth century. The legal principles upon which deposit banking was based were still in existence, carried over from the earlier Roman law. This rebirth and the welcome it received through Europe testify to the growing demand for insured safety and a capital market to lower the costs of financing commerce.

Insurance too had its beginnings during this period, associated – as one would expect – with the expansion of maritime commerce; its prime movers were the Italians. At this time the typical coverage was not complete, but insured only a percentage of the value of the cargo. The earliest known examples of insurance loans date from 1287, in a founding deed drafted by a notary in Palermo. Later their use spread to other cities, extending the use of the market mechanism to spread risks. The success of insurance in at least partially securing trade ventures led, even in such early days, to the eventual extension of coverage to many other activities where actuarily determined risks permitted such institutional innovation.

The creation of other institutions to facilitate the extension of credit followed the inception of deposit banking. Ingenious minds devised various bills of exchange and forms of direct loans to underwrite long-distance transactions, as well as mechanisms for the collection and repayment of these loans. The number and size of regional fairs increased as it became evident that these localized marts could bridge the distances between widely separated sellers and buyers and simplify their financial dealings. In effect, the fair was a primitive organized market where sellers, gathered in one place during a specified period of time, could attract buyers.

The Champagne Fairs, centrally established in France during the twelfth and thirteenth centuries, played a prominent role in the commerce between Southern and Northern Europe. A cycle of six fairs eventually evolved there, making this area almost a year-round center for the commerce of Western Europe and the meeting ground between the North and South. As goods in considerable and growing quantities were exchanged, the fairs became both a major market for international trade and a center of an embryonic international capital market, providing an organized and

---

[5] See *Cambridge Economic History*, vol. 3, pp. 49–52, for further discussion. The investor also assumed only limited liability, thereby further reducing the risks of such an undertaking. The sea loan was still another form of contractual arrangement for maritime undertakings. *Ibid.*, pp. 53–8.

systematic locus for international credit transactions and the mechanism to make payments. A market evolved there for exchanging currencies, with ratios quoted on the basis of 1 sou or 12 derniers of Provins, equal to some amount of a foreign currency. This was in effect a freely fluctuating exchange rate which mirrored the demand and supply of different European currencies, reflecting the international balance of payments between the trading areas. The institutional instrument devised for transactions (known as an *instrumentum ex causa cambii*) permitted a borrower who had received an advance in local currency to promise repayment in another currency, at another place. This prototype of a bill of exchange was a significant contribution to the general lowering of transaction costs in international trade that occurred during the century. It allowed an easily transported and hidden piece of paper to replace the more costly to transport and secure metallic money as a means of payment in exchanges.

It is important once more to emphasize the productivity consequence of these institutional innovations. The manorial world of relatively isolated economic units, or even the larger regional aggregations like the towns of Flanders and the Netherlands, did not at the beginning of the century have continuous information about relative prices and the underlying supply and demand conditions for their own geographic areas, let alone for foreign dealings. Transactions were too infrequent in time and space to support an organized market. During the thirteenth century this vacuum was filled initially by fairs, which served as a major institutional arrangement to provide such information. To a growing extent, they replaced the sporadic and expensive medieval practice of ascertaining by haggling the unique exchange relationships for each transaction. Because of their growing volume, the fairs thus provided generalized knowledge of prices for an international market, reducing the costly search by individuals for market information, and played an equally pioneering role in the development of a capital market by developing effective credit instruments. Every one of these innovations reduced transaction costs; the fairs, like other institutional innovations described earlier, were sources of productivity increase.

The periodic fairs began to decline in the thirteenth century, increasingly replaced by permanent markets located in centrally placed urban areas, a process which had occurred earlier in Italy. The fate of the Champagne Fair provides an interesting illustration. The absorption of the Champagne district into the kingdom of France had subjected the district and the Fair to heavy royal taxation. Meanwhile, the opening of a direct sea route from Italy to the Low Countries during the last quarter of the century reduced the transport costs of an alternate route between the North and South.

The provision of market information is subject to economies of scale. Once a transaction has been arranged, the price and conditions of the exchange provide information about market conditions. The transaction cost *per merchant* declines as the information is disseminated among increasing numbers. The average and marginal cost of information is thus lowered as the size of the market grows, and in the primitive but thriving market economy of the thirteenth century, with trade growing apace in all directions, we would expect to see a permanent international market develop in a centrally located place. This might have been the destiny of the Champagne district, had not royal taxation penalized the Champagne Fairs at the same crucial period when a new direct sea route had just been opened up between Italy and the Low Countries. That combination of events allowed Bruges to emerge as the most important market west of the Alps.[6]

Urban markets like Bruges now welcomed the organizations and institutions which were already employed by the fairs to facilitate international commerce. The Italians had provided the leadership in establishing these secondary institutional arrangements discussed above (and numerous others as well), but the Northern Europeans, first in regional fairs then in a permanent interregional urban market, were quick to follow suit. Those new institutional arrangements involved the setting up of formal contractual arrangements to replace the earlier informal agreements – that is, they were specified forms of property rights which delineated permissible methods of co-operation and competition. Of necessity, then, their enforcement required the sanction of law.

Much of the body of commercial law which now evolved had its origins in the customs of merchants, and it was only gradually codified as a result of increasing literacy during the century. Explicit written laws for the enforcement of trade agreements first appeared, as might have been expected, in the towns and fairs where trade and commerce were prospering. Since the Italian cities were in the forefront of this commercial development, they led in the formalization of legal forms. However, the booming international commerce made it inevitable that principles governing trade in any important area would be assimilated and incorporated in overall laws governing interregional trade.

A major fraction of commercial law was the development of rules of conduct with respect to debts and the enforcement of contracts. These procedures came to be sustained either by reciprocal agreement or, within the area of the market, by merchant tribunals which lay outside the feudal ecclesiastical courts. As commerce spread, so did the fundamental commercial customs. Thus the maritime law of Pisa served as a model for that of Barcelona, which in turn reappears as the codified *charte d'Oleron*, in the beginning of the thirteenth century, subsequently serving as the model for developing commercial law in the Netherlands and in England.

To experience the benefits of an expanding market, a region had to be

[6] J. A. Van Houtte, 'The Rise and Decline of the Market of Bruges'. *The Economic History Review* (April 1966), 29–48.

aware of the stable and fundamental laws upon which the existence of commerce is based, and to be in accord with other areas on their consistent enforcement. The obvious benefits to a region of expanding its market activity made the existing powers eager to uphold and spread such a rule of law, whether the government was controlled by a king, the nobility, or (in the growing towns and cities) by a merchant oligarchy. Regardless of who held the purse-strings, profits would accrue from safe, orderly and legally protected trade routes, market sites, and contract agreements.

However, since these profitable new arrangements could be enforced only by legal sanctions which required the coercive power of government for their support, it was a fact of life that part of the created profits must therefore go to the policing authority in return for its efforts and sanctions. The expansion of trade obviously involved a changed distribution of income among the classes of feudal society. How the gains from trade would be divided was a source of dispute. As an example of the quarrels induced among members of society as to how the gains should be distributed: the number of local tolls on the Rhine River increased from nineteen in the year 1200 to more than thirty-five in the year 1300. But, however distributed, the gains remained substantial.

The blossoming of international fairs and of urban centers to facilitate interregional commerce was meanwhile being paralleled by the appearance of local boroughs and fairs. These humbler marketplaces collected regional produce for export, distributed imported goods, and facilitated the exchange of locally produced goods within the area. While it is possible that the expansion of civic populations during this period lagged somewhat behind that of the country as a whole, towns did grow absolutely both in size and in numbers. In England, as elsewhere, the founding of new towns and fairs was encouraged by the Crown and by major nobles who sold the legal rights to hold markets and to establish guilds.

Towns rose during the thirteenth century primarily for mercantile rather than for manufacturing reasons. Nevertheless, crafts were becoming more firmly established in the urban centers as the bustling medieval trader began to discover that he could get goods of better quality in towns than on the manor, because specialization made possible by the larger market resulted in more skillful workmanship.

Having proved its worth by producing better goods, specialization itself was now in process of hardening into occupational guilds. At its inception, the medieval guild purchased from the existing coercive power (the Crown, a major lord, or the town burgesses) the exclusive right to practice a certain trade within a given area. These early-day monopolists, the members of the guild, exploited their position for the benefit of the membership, often standing together as security for loans of working capital, as well as setting standards of quality and (often) restricting the quantity of output.

The work that members of any guild could perform was more limited or specialized the larger the market area in which it sold its wares. The expansion of the textile industry in the Low Countries, for example, saw the development of highly specialized guilds, with Flemish textile regulations separating into many distinct trades the various processes through which raw wool became cloth. Virgin wool was sorted and graded by women in a warehouse. After the larger pieces of dirt were removed by men, the wool was put out to other women, working in their homes, for washing, combing, spinning and sizing. Next it was turned over to men for weaving, then sent to the fulling trough. After that, it was given to the dyers and finally subjected to several more finishing processes before the cloth was ready for sale. Each step was governed by a separate guild.

So efficient was this extensive division of labor that, abetted by the increasingly efficient market system, it enabled Flemish cloth to undercut the prices of any less specialized local clothmaking guilds throughout Europe. England's infant textile industry was particularly damaged as the lower-priced Flemish cloth draped the booths of more and more local fairs. Skillful Flemish immigrants had actually helped at the birth of the English textile industry in the twelfth century and English guilds of weavers had existed in the larger textile towns before 1150; but they had concentrated upon producing for local markets and the imported Flemish cloth now shattered the local monopolies these guilds had enjoyed. The result was to force English cloth production out of the monopolized towns and into the unregulated countryside – partly to escape the costly restrictions of the local guilds, partly to utilize water to power the fulling mills. In others parts of Europe, some industries were located in the countryside for a more direct reason: the mining of such raw materials as gold, silver, copper, iron, tin and lead gained importance during the century, although because of the primitive state of technology the costs of extraction increased significantly as soon as the diggings went deep enough to hit water. During the latter part of the century, mining in general suffered diminishing returns.

As a share of the gross regional product of most areas during the thirteenth century, manufacturing remained less important than agriculture and probably than commerce. The market, however, dominated the patterns of production. Mercantile interests extended credit and decidedly influenced, if they did not actually dictate, the manufacturing processes themselves. In quantitative terms the working capital thus provided was more important than the fixed physical capital employed in manufacturing. Manufacture generally continued to be heavily labor-intensive and subject to constant returns to scale, the only exceptions being the extractive industries of mining and metallurgy, where increasing costs were experienced in expanding output.

The gains to the societies of Medieval Europe during the thirteenth century stemming from the growth of commerce were substantial. The cost of using the market to allocate resources declined significantly. The result was the increased gains from specialization as the market widened. Trade between Western and Southern Europe became regular and continuous. Specialized areas of manufacture and trade such as Flanders and Bruges developed. Other areas specialized in products such as wheat, wine, wool and timber.

It is perhaps easy to make too much of these developments for the vast majority of the labor force of Western Europe was still engaged directly upon the land. We have already learned that it was the decline in productivity during the thirteenth century of this, the dominant sector, that accounts for the gloom of succeeding centuries. The question that must be considered is why the reduction in the cost of using the market did not generate increases in productivity in this sector as it did in commerce and manufacturing.

The answer is that in some ways it did, but these gains were not sufficient to offset the decline in productivity that a continually growing population created. Agriculture in general experienced diminishing returns to an ever-expanding labor force, a condition that did not burden industry or commerce. When diminishing returns are present and the labor force grows, the productivity of the industry as well as its labor force will decline. Such a decline is assured unless the gains from trade, improvements in organization and technological changes occur in sufficient amounts to offset the loss due to diminishing returns. There is no doubt that some gains in efficiency were achieved in the agriculture sector by increased specialization. The specialization of different areas in wheat, wool and wine, reported above, certainly brought to the producer some of the gains from trade. A much wider range of consumption goods of higher quality was available if one produced for the market than if one attempted to be self-sufficient.

While the spread of the market allowed some gains from specialization, the opposite appears to have been the case with the efficiency of organization. There appears to have been a tendency to return the demesne to direct cultivation by the lord, using the forced labor owed to him by his unfree tenants. The previous trend toward fixed money rents and the annual commutation of labor dues for a fixed money payment was reversed on some manors. In its place we see the return to the traditional manorial organization.

The reason for this reversal is not difficult to ascertain. After the lands of the frontier and between manors had all been taken up, the continued growth in population significantly altered, as we have seen, the value of labor relative to land. The owners of rights to land now held a more valuable possession; the owners of labor, a less valuable one. Such a drastic change in factor prices required a revision in manorial contracts to match the new relative scarcities, but to avoid costly complications the alteration in payments had to be set within the framework of existing customs. The lord had an added incentive to change the terms because inflation had significantly reduced the real value of the fixed money payments he had previously been receiving, yet the customs of the manor regarded these payments as unchanging. (Indeed, the very word 'farm' stems from the word meaning 'fixed'.) The frequent renegotiation of a rent payment and a commutation payment under conditions of inflation would have proved very costly, entailing little less than a complete break with tradition, the governing law of the manor.

The landlord's quandary during the thirteenth century was therefore twofold: he had to deal with the problems of a rising price level which reduced the real value of his money income, at the same time that the augmented value of his land brought about by expanding population was producing gains – not for him – but for his tenants, under the prevailing fixed rates. From the lord's point of view, the establishment of a fixed crop rent or a sharecrop would have dealt adequately with the problem of inflation by itself. But to cope with the rising real value of land would have required periodic renegotiation in favor of his share – a costly process within the institutional structure of the thirteenth century manorial economy. In view of such difficulties, it was often less expensive for the lord to exercise his acknowledged right by returning the demesne to his own direct cultivation, rather than to attempt frequent renegotiation of the terms of exchange under an existing contract.

Such reasoning thus explains the seeming paradox of a return to labor dues as the means of cultivating the demesne in the presence of a market economy and in the face of the declining real value of labor. The value of labor was obviously much lower than during the twelfth century, when the amount of the fixed commutation payment had been established. Yet the lords often chose to claim labor dues, in spite of their lower real value, rather than to continue accepting the offsetting money payment and to hire free laborers. This transition apparently occurred over wide areas despite the abundance of peasants whose land holdings were insufficient to permit them to be totally employed on their own holdings, and despite the notorious shirking problems encountered with forced labor.

This suggests the possibility that due to inflation the money price of free labor increased, despite the decline in its real value to the point where wages were greater than the fixed commutation payments, in which case lords would choose to reclaim labor obligations. Perhaps we should not over-emphasize the extent of the return to labor dues. The evidence is not sufficient to estimate how commonly this happened, only to establish that some manors did revert to labor dues.

Where fixed rents and commutation payments survived, it is likely that the lords took other steps to adjust to the changing relative and absolute price levels. Under such conditions, it is probable that the lords, where possible, stepped up the required payments to bring them more into line with the change in relative factor prices. It is also not surprising to discover that the lords augmented and collected every payment that was their acknowledged right. Serfs and customary tenants, who together made up a majority of the people in agriculture, were increasingly considered unfree and could not leave their holdings without losing them. Nor could they generally buy or sell their rights to their holdings without the lord's permission. Furthermore, they had to have the Lord's permission to marry off a daughter or sometimes even a son. Death dues were collected (the heriot and mortuary) and ever-increasing entry fines were required from heirs before they could take possession of the holding. Besides labor dues, an annual rent was often paid plus, in certain places, the tallage, a household tax. In other places a license had to be obtained before the peasant could even sell his livestock.

Each of these restrictions, which increasingly burdened the villein during the thirteenth century, was a part of the means used by the lords to capture the increasing value of land. A restriction was designed either to increase as the land rose in value, or else to make sure that the lord would actually collect his due. The restrictions on movement and sale, for example, were to ensure that the heriot and mortuary were collectable. Permissions were, of course, also a source of revenue when the lord chose to grant them. The entry fine which could be increased captured to some extent the rise in the value of land. The various licenses and permissions which could be varied according to the wealth of the villein were another means.

Thus, the burdens of villeinage were the means used to increase the payments to the owners of rights in land relative to the payments to labor. Each burden was the acknowledged right of the lord, guaranteed by the customs of the manor. In total these burdens could not exceed the economic value of the holding or the tenant would give it up. It was more efficient to augment and increase these payments than to create a new mechanism to adjust to the changing situation which initially would be in conflict with the fundamental institutions of the manor.

Unfortunately, implicit in the basic restrictions of villeinage were important implications for the efficiency with which agriculture could be organized. The inability to alienate land freely and the tightening restrictions on labor movement were obvious hindrances to the efficient allocation of resources. The inability of the efficient peasant to obtain more land easily and of the inefficient peasant to easily dispose of some of his holdings reduced the overall efficiency of agriculture in general. Even if legal subterfuges were employed these could only be used at increased cost. The restrictions on the movement of labor from labor-rich areas to labor-poor ones had the same effect. The tax on permission to sell livestock discouraged specialization in stock raising. The annual tallage and the necessity to pay to obtain various permissions, where the payment was apt to vary with the affluence of the peasant, were discouraging to the accumulation of wealth and capital.

The obligations of serfdom thus discouraged the efficient allocation of resources in the dominant agricultural sector. The fact that what a peasant had and what he made were going to be shared with his immediate lord raised the value of leisure above its true social value. The peasant was encouraged to spend too little effort in productive activities.

The revival of labor dues, which, as we have seen above, was due to changing prices during the period, had equally disastrous consequences for the overall efficiency of the agricultural sector. The tendency for labor dues to be increasingly employed to farm the demesne lands transferred an increasing portion of the agricultural labor force to work under a system that encouraged shirking, required close supervision, and reduced further the productivity of labor already substantially reduced by the abundance of labor relative to land.

Bad as these changes were – as difficult as they made it for the agricultural sector to adjust efficiently to altered conditions – they were not the only hindrance to increasing the productivity of the agricultural sector. We have seen that the peasant had little incentive to increase his productivity, hence his wealth, for the lord would obtain much of whatever gains resulted. Nor could the peasant improve his lot by flight, for this condition was general. The owners of particular rights to land – the lords – were the ones who could gain from increasing the productivity of agriculture.

The lords, however, because they were many, had little individual incentive either to alter the form of their extortions or to engage in research or to promote innovations. The costs of changing the fundamental institutional arrangements of the manor were substantial. Not all peasants would gain by any change and even the augmentation within the existing system of rules had brought discontent and minor uprisings. Since no lord could capture even a small portion of the social product of improved agricultural processes and technology, each had little incentive to try. The rational response would be to wait for some other landowner to bear the research and development costs and then to simply imitate his procedures should they prove successful. Each lord, of course, chose to wait and little progress was made.

However, not all the institutional changes in the agricultural sector ran counter to increasing efficiency. The increasing economic value of land, for instance, led to fundamental changes in land law in England. These changes affected freeholders only, not serfs. While it is not known what percentage of English lands were freely held in the thirteenth century, it is clear that they comprised only a minority of the total. The land held by freemen, those whose services to the lord were fixed and specified, gradually over the century became freely alienable.

This was not yet possible in Glanvil's time (the 1180s) and subterfuges in the form of leases were used to transfer land. By the end of the thirteenth century, however, freeholders had acquired the right to sell land by substitution, the buyer taking the place of the seller for consideration. Thus an important clause in one definition of private property – the right to enjoy and the right to alienate – was established in English law. Even if it applied to only a minority of English lands, the precedent was of tremendous importance.

This development in the history of property rights did not come about without substantial controversy. The rising real value of land provided incentives to establish, re-establish, and define the claims to land by rival groups in the society. Two key statutes in this regard were: Merton in 1235 and Westminster in 1285. These permitted the manorial lord to enclose wasteland so long as sufficient land was left for the tenants. Thus the lords obtained the exclusive right to substantial areas of the manor's land formerly belonging to all of the inhabitants.

One of the key elements in this continuing dispute was the right to transfer land. Feudal law did not recognize the concept of land ownership. Its basic characteristic was that several persons had jurisdiction or held and shared particular rights to the same piece of land. The king, the tenants *in capite*, the mesne tenants, and the tenants paravail (or, more simply, the king, the lords, and the peasants) each held particular rights to receive income, called incidents, from the land.

There existed two ways to transfer land, by substitution or by sub-infeudation. The former required that the land be surrendered to the lord who in turn granted the land to another, and the second, that the tenant in turn grant the land to another, the tenant becoming the lord of the person to whom he conveyed the land. The incidents or obligations of the land remained in either case. Sub-infeudation, however, added another tenant to the feudal chain. The lord, in the event of a dispute, could move only against his tenant and not his tenant's tenant. Should his tenant disappear, the higher lords were apt to lose their incidents since they had no legal recourse against the person actually in possession of the land.

This was particularly apt to happen if the tenant was a freeman. So concerned were the lords with this problem that the restatement of the Great Charter in 1217 stipulated: 'No free men shall henceforth give or seil so much of his land that the residue shall be insufficient to support the services due in respect to the fee.' A succession of actions brought in the King's Court during the thirteenth century gradually permitted alienation by substitution between free men without the mesne lord's permission. The Statute *Quia emptores* in 1290 only confirmed what had become established practice. This act specifically forbade sub-infeudation. Interestingly, this right was not extended to tenants in chief until 1327.

It is revealing to inquire how the freeholders in England acquired the right to alienate their lands in sum, obtaining a property right approaching fee-simple ownership. The Norman conquest had resulted in a stronger central government in England than existed in the rest of the feudal world. The centralized authority of the King's Court in England had no exact parallel on the Continent. During the thirteenth century the King's Court gradually expanded its jurisdiction relative to the seigneurial courts. One of the key precedents that emerged from this struggle was the recognition that the King's Court held jurisdiction over free men. A freeman came to be defined as a man whose obligations were strictly defined. As the manorial lords lost jurisdiction over the freeman, they also lost control over his land holdings. These favorable developments in England were unique in the feudal world. Elsewhere, except in the Netherlands, the legal institutions still did not recognize exclusive property rights in land. The revival and application of Roman law on the Continent, particularly in Germany, did not afford the lessee legal protection. The tenant was subject to arbitrary eviction and the hereditary lease was not allowed. The development of private property in land on the continent thus generally lagged behind England during the thirteenth century.

IV

The growth of population and the resultant expansion of organized markets and a money economy changed the basic conditions which had given rise to feudal society. In previous sections of this chapter we have seen some of the consequences for the private sectors, both agricultural and non-agricultural. It had equally revolutionary consequences for the public sector. We have viewed feudalism as a contractual fiscal relationship in which labor services were exchanged for protection and justice. Local lords provided superior lords and ultimately the king with knights for the protection of the realm. At the bottom of the social ladder villeins and free labor produced the goods and services for the society. The manor was the focal point for this contractual relationship even though the hierarchy ran up to the greatest lord – the king. We have seen that in the classic feudal era, protection and justice were predominantly the province of the local lord. By 1300 this relationship was changing, but we should note carefully that even at that date the local manorial lord was still the predominant dispenser of justice and, in some areas, of protection. In England the freeman had come under the protection of the King's Court, but the villein was still subject to the manorial court. Moreover, outside the manor, the growing boroughs and towns were often self-governing and provided local justice and military protection themselves. It remained true that the towns generally had an overlord who was the ultimate protection against major military and political threats.

But although public goods were still predominantly local, the thirteenth century pointed the way towards pervasive changes. The sources of change were two: (1) the growth of trade and the increasing demand for the protection of private property in long-distance trade; and (2) the consequences of a money economy upon the minimum efficient size of military units.

Trade outside the boundary of a local manor was only possible if protection were provided – something beyond the ability of any local lord. The growing potential gains from trade encouraged the growth of order on a larger scale. Merchants going to the Champagne Fairs, for example, were guaranteed safe conduct by the count of Champagne and the king of France. Alien merchants were given trading privileges and many towns were guaranteed freedom of trade – all symptomatic of a widening of protection beyond the local manor. Indeed, the burgeoning trade of the thirteenth century described above would have been impossible without the extension of protection on a larger scale. It is true that caravans going to the Champagne Fairs were employed for protection and heavily armed as late as the early thirteenth century, but increasingly the locus of protection had shifted from individuals and the manor to regional courts and barons, and even to kings of larger areas. Thus the protection of private property rights over goods in long-distance trade was a powerful stimulus toward the growth of larger political organizations. As the functions of regional and national governments expanded during the thirteenth century so did their fiscal requirements.

The second source of change was military. In the era of classic feudalism, a local lord owed his superior lord so many knights for military service, usually forty days a year. After that, the knights went home. Large-scale extended warfare under such circumstances was difficult. The development of a money economy had brought with it scutage – the payment of money instead of labor inputs (knight service). The king was now in the position of being able to hire a standing or temporary army. While the heyday of large mercenary armies was still in the future, mercenaries were increasingly employed in the thirteenth century. The ultimate result was to make possible larger-scale and more prolonged warfare. It also weakened the power of vassals in relationship to the Crown, thereby increasing the king's *de facto* authority over potentially recalcitrant vassals.

The extension of state protection to property in trade and the employment of larger military forces were both costly. Where did the Crown or the barons get the increased revenues? The revenue sources of the French and English Crown at the beginning of the thirteenth century (1202–3) were as follows:

> The first constituent of the revenue of the king of France in that year consisted of the payments of the *prevots* and *baillis*, amounting to about 60,000 li. par. after certain fixed local charges were met. This sum was derived from the issues of the royal forests and agricultural domains, a variety of seignorial rights, and the profits of justice, markets, ecclesiastical patronage, etc. In addition, the king received certain extraordinary payments directly related to the emergency of war – payments from non-nobles and vavassors for the commutation of military service, a *taille* levied on the domain and contributions exacted from towns, churches, and Jews in the domain – amounting in all to about 63,000 li. par. The English revenues of King John two years later were in the region of £20,000, derived in the main from the farms of shires and boroughs, the proceeds of feudal escheats and incidents, the issues of ecclesiastical estates in hand during vacancies and the profits of royal justice. On that occasion, however, the total also included part of the proceeds of a scutage and of fines for the commutation of military service and of a tallage levied on the domain and the Jews, which in aggregate produced in this and the following year a sum of about £6,900. King John also succeeded in imposing duties on trade in 1202 and levying general taxes on moveables 1203 and 1207, the last yielding the astonishing amount of £57,000. The customs were soon abandoned however, and like the tax on movables, represented merely the first harbingers of the fiscal system of the future.[7]

We can see that the bulk of the revenues still came from the traditional feudal incidents of the Crown; from its estates and the various feudal obligations of lesser lords. But some, as noted in the quotation, were harbingers of the future. The *Taille*, a form of direct taxation, became a mainstay of French fiscal policy as did the customs in England. Special or annual assessment of Jews and foreign merchants, tolls and the granting of monopoly privileges were common, if minor, sources of revenue at this time. We should particularly note one feature. Sometimes the Crown was forced to call together assemblages of propertied groups in order to obtain a special levy from them. These were the beginnings of representative bodies. Such convocations frequently received privileges and the delegation of authority in exchange for their permission to be taxed. In succeeding centuries, we shall see that the gradual evolution of English parliamentary control over fiscal matters stemmed from these beginnings.

Thus, at the beginning of the thirteenth century the Crown enjoyed

[7] *Cambridge Economic History*, vol. 3, pp. 302–3.

diverse sources of revenue but they were still predominantly feudal in origin. Indeed, frequently, much of the Crown's revenue was still in *kind*. The count of Flanders was still forced to move his court from one location to another to consume the taxes in kind. Also, the Crown was always hard-pressed for revenue. The demands placed upon these governments grew more rapidly than feudal revenues. Every potential source of income was explored; from territorial acquisitions such as those made by the dukes of Burgundy and the king of France during the century, to more efficient administration of their estates and outright confiscation.

In spite of ever-growing needs, the barons and kings had to be careful not to press their subjects too hard, for it was ever possible that those whose wealth or income was too adversely affected would revolt. The concessions in the Great Charter, as well as in charters won by the leagues of early fourteenth-century France testified that this type of opposition was real. By the end of the thirteenth century, the requirements of the Crown and regional governments had increased astronomically while the traditional sources of fiscal revenue from feudal incidents were either not growing or else actually declining.

The important right to alienate land was affected by the fiscal crisis. The right to alienate, for example, was granted by the Crown; in France by Philip Augustus in 1210, by the Statute of *Quia emptores* in England, and in Champagne and elsewhere to protect crown revenues. The problem was everywhere the same, relative to the requirements, feudal revenues were on the wane. New sources of revenues were needed. We can see the contrast with the early thirteenth century by examining English and French fiscal receipts at the end of the century.

The age of Edward I and Philip the Fair saw extraordinary levies become more frequent, more general in their incidences and more indispensable. In England under Edward I taxation of the Church provided some £200,000 towards the King's needs. General parliamentary taxes on movables yielded a further £500,000, and a national customs-system was established. In 1275 export duties were imposed on wool, wool-fells, and hides; the rates were augmented for a time in 1294–97, and in 1303 additional export and import duties were negotiated with the alien merchants trading to England. The average yield of the custom of 1275 for the years 1275–94 and 1299–1304 was about £10,000 yearly, and revenue from taxes on trade must have been higher in 1294–97 and in the last years of the reign after the new charges imposed on alien commerce had come into operation. In all, Edward I raised £1,000,000 or more in the course of his reign by direct and indirect taxation.

Philip the Fair of France had no less need of taxes. Like Edward, he laid the clergy under frequent contribution. On the other hand, he encountered more formidable obstacles in his attempts to establish general direct taxation, and the resultant story is one of empiricism and improvisation. Many experiments were tried, including taxes on income from property or chattels, hearth taxes, the commutation of military obligations imposed *ad hoc* on the different classes and communities, and feudal aids extended to include rear vassals. Some of these levies yielded notable sums: the subsidy of 1295 possibly 350,000 to 360,000 li. par., and that of 1304 700,000 li. tur. or more, though in a depreciated currency. At the same time, they became progressively more difficult to raise. The king was compelled to accept in their place special compositions with individual towns and communities; and as early as 1295 had to buy the acquiescence of the nobility by conceding to them a share of the taxes levied on their domains. Direct taxation, therefore, had to be supplemented by other methods of raising revenue. A tax on sales was imposed in 1291; but it provided a riot in Rouen, towns and provinces bought exemption from it, and it was abandoned in 1295 (though similar charges were imposed in 1296, 1314, and under Charles IV). The Jews were tallaged time and time again, 44,000 li. tur. being taken from them in the years 1298–1301 alone; and eventually they were expelled for a time and their property seized in 1306. Italian merchant-financiers were compelled to buy from the king immunity from spoliation, receipts from this source amounting to 221,000 li. tur. in 1291–92 and 65,000 li. tur. in 1295. Forced loans were raised and not always repaid. Manipulation of the currency on a massive scale was perhaps the most important financial expedient of all: 1,200,000 li. tur. was procured by this means in 1298–99, about two thirds of the total receipts of the treasury.[8]

This lengthy quotation makes clear how the sources of revenue had changed. The clergy, a major holder of wealth in the medieval world, was a prime source. We see the contrast between the levying of customs duties in England and local taxation of feudal demesnes (however with the important feature of a kickback to the local lord) in France. The taxation of alien merchants and Jews, and currency debasement added to the sources of revenue.

By the mid-thirteenth century, European rulers' fiscal needs during wartime had outstripped their regular revenues to such an extent that heavy and sustained borrowing was their only recourse. In the beginning of the century, lending was infrequent. When it did occur, the loan was secured by a pledge of land and the lender was frequently ecclesiastical. During the century the frequency and nature of loans to governments changed. The revenues of the Crown from taxes or customs duties were pledged and the

[8] *Ibid.*, p. 304.

lenders *par excellence* were Italian (although earlier the Flemish had played a role, as did some local creditors). Thus the Riccardi of Luca lent Edward I (for the conquest of Wales and other military expenses) £392,000 between 1272 and 1294. It was the custom of kings to farm out their revenues. The customs were placed in the lenders' hands during that period as a source of repayment. The Riccardi were succeeded by the Frescobaldi of Florence who played the same role. The French, to provide another example, in the thirteenth century borrowed from the Order of the Templars in Paris. In 1287 Philip the Fair owed the Temple 101,000 Li. par. (about one-sixth of annual royal revenues). The count of Flanders, as another example, had readily at hand the substantial financial resources of the rich towns such as Ghent from which to borrow or tax.

The history of royal lending, however, was fraught with peril for the lender and many a financier and banking house then as well as later went bankrupt as a result of royal default. The rate of interest, reflecting the high risk, correspondingly became very high. We shall see in subsequent chapters how the public and private capital market was influenced by princely financing.

V

We are now in a position to begin to summarize our answer to the question posed at the beginning of this chapter. Why did thirteenth-century Europe not break out of the Malthusian trap? The answer lies in the nature of the property rights that developed, or failed to develop, during this century.

The creation and enforcement of property rights are a prerogative of the government as the source of coercion. The locus of governmental coercion and decision-making shifted from local to larger political units. This movement was slow and halting, for everywhere it was circumscribed by conflicting authority. So even when the short-run fiscal interests of government coincided with the development of more efficient property rights (as in the protection of long-distance trade, which provided a new source of crown revenue) because of conflicts with rivals it frequently could produce only imperfect methods of enforcement. The most important causal factor in the development of new property rights was the fact that the government created them only when it was in its fiscal interest. As we saw above, the granting of the alienability of land (a key step in the development of fee-simple absolute ownership) was accomplished in England, France, Anjou, Poiters and other areas to ensure that the Crown would not lose existing feudal revenues. Protection of the property rights of alien merchants had a similar origin, as did the Burgundian establishment of fairs at Autun and Chalon. For identical reasons counter-productive actions, such as the multiplication of tolls, arbitrary confiscation, forced loans and many other similar devices, were taken, which made for greater uncertainty with respect to property rights. The direction the government took depended upon its fiscal interest.

While the secondary institutional arrangements which had arisen with the expansion of trade and commerce and the development of greater exclusive rights in agricultural land had led to productivity increase, they were not sufficient to allow output to outstrip population growth. It should be evident from the above description that they were piecemeal, frequently arbitrarily given and often just as arbitrarily withdrawn. Trade and commerce were protected only when their promotion suited the lords' and the Crown's interest; frequently they were impeded or hindered for the same reason.

We have discussed above the reasons why the agricultural sector did not increase its productivity at a pace sufficient to overcome the decline due to diminishing returns and a growing population. What we have not discussed is why population continued to expand in the face of declining incomes.

As population grew, and general diminishing returns set in, there were rising social costs to a family having more children. But these social costs were different from the private costs borne by the individual family who might find it still to their advantage to have more children. Indeed, the thirteenth-century family had only very imperfect ways of preventing the birth of additional children. It is true that there were always practices which tended to discourage large families in periods of falling real income. We know of the tendency for marriages to be delayed and for some primitive forms of contraception to be employed. These methods clearly were imperfect, and in the face of the inability to have effective contraception or to devise effective social control, the tendency for population to grow was inexorable.

In order for productivity on a sustained basis to outstrip the growth of population, it was necessary that the social and private rates of return on all activities move closer together. This occurred in industry and trade during the thirteenth century, but did not occur in the dominant agricultural sector. Especially in the important area of invention and innovations, institutions did not develop to bring the social and private rates closer together. The result was that the rate of population growth was greater than the rate of economic progress.

However, it would leave an inaccurate impression to close this chapter on such a dismal note. We have already noted that fundamental institutional arrangements change very slowly, and many persisted and survived the harsh fourteenth century. When population began to grow again, they provided a fundamental base for further institutional innovation.

7. THE FOURTEENTH AND FIFTEENTH CENTURIES

The fourteenth and fifteenth centuries suffered contractions, crisis and perhaps even depression. The regions of Europe were repeatedly visited by famine, pestilence, war and revolution. Population declined in the wake of these catastrophes, turning the economic and social order upside down. This was a 'hateful time' for most of its inhabitants, but not all. This was the time of the Renaissance – a rebirth of artistic and intellectual achievements. In short, it is difficult to give a simple assessment of these centuries.

I

However, the general contours of this era are clear. The phenomenon that weighed most heavily upon the period was the absolute decline in population. All historians agree on this, but that is about as far as their agreement goes. It is not known for certain exactly when the population of Western Europe began to fall, how severe a decline occurred, nor when the population began to recover.

The main reason for the uncertainty lies in the dearth of statistical evidence. In these pre-census years, any estimate of total population can be little better than guesswork. Several estimates do exist and two are presented here, for what they are worth. M. K. Bennett has constructed estimates of the population of Europe. These are presented in Table 7.1. A more detailed estimate exists for England alone, constructed by J. C. Russell, an authority on medieval demography. His estimates are found in

TABLE 7.1   *The Population of Western Europe: 1200–1550*

Year	Population (millions)	Year	Population (millions)
1200	61	1400	45
1250	69	1450	60
1300	73	1500	69
1350	51	1550	78

Source: M. K. Bennett, *The World's Food* (1954), p. 5.

TABLE 7.2   *The Population of England: 1086–1603*

Year	Population	Year	Population
1086	1,100,000	1374	2,250,000
1348	3,757,500	1377	2,223,373
1350	3,127,500	1400	2,100,000
1360–61	2,745,000	1430	2,100,000
1369	2,452,500	1603	3,780,000

Source: J. C. Russell, *British Medieval Populations* (1948), pp. 248, 263, and 269–70.

Table 7.2. Russell's estimates suggests that the English population declined substantially during the second half of the fourteenth century and had not yet begun to recover by 1430. Indeed, it was not until the beginning of the seventeenth century that the population of England exceeded the level of 1348.

It is obvious that even if the above estimates are accurate they are too gross to answer the major questions asked above. It is possible, however, to suggest an interpretation. Death's executioners are traditionally considered to be '*fama, pestus et bellum*' – famine, pestilence and war. Each individually or in the company of his fellows visited Western Europe repeatedly during the fourteenth and fifteenth centuries. When and how often did these grim visitors come?

The fourteenth century was only one decade old when the first of several Malthusian checks occurred. Between 1315 and 1317 Europe experienced a general famine which, like many famines, was also accompanied by epidemic. It was neither the first famine to hit during the fourteenth century nor the last. In France, famines were recorded in 1304, 1305, 1310, 1315, 1322, 1325, 1330–4, 1344, 1349–51, 1358–61, 1371, 1374–5 and 1390. In addition, Southern France suffered the following years of scarcity: 1312, 1313, 1323, 1329, 1335–6, 1337, 1343 and 1361. England fared somewhat better, recording famines during the following years: 1315–16, 1321, 1351 and 1369. Food shortage was an ever-present danger to the population of fourteenth-century Europe; no area was completely immune. When famine occurred the results could be terrible. On one occasion, 10 percent of the cloth-manufacturing town of Ypres and 5.5 percent of the population of Bruges died of starvation.

Famine often set the stage for disease, if it was not actually accompanied by it. The most spectacular occurrence during 1348–51 was the Black Death – the bubonic and pneumonic plague – which began in the Crimea, spread across Europe, and swept by 1350 throughout Northern Europe following the routes of merchants and shepherds. Nor did the plague strike only once, but returned again and again. In Spain the plague recurred in 1362–3, 1371, 1375, 1381, 1396, 1397, continuing on into the fifteenth century in 1410, 1429, 1439, 1448, 1465–6, 1476, 1483, 1486, 1493–4 and 1497. Fortunately, not every country suffered as often as Spain, but the danger of plague was ever-present. In England the plague returned in 1368–9 and again in 1374. In London alone the plague returned twenty times during the fifteenth century.

How large was the population decline associated with the Black Death; not only with the Great Plague of 1347–51, but with the successive plagues? We will never know for sure. First of all, the plagues' incidence was very different in different areas; some suffering mortality in excess of 50 percent of the population, others being almost completely unaffected and some avoiding the plague altogether. The classic view was that the plague carried away approximately one-third of the population of Europe, but subsequent researchers have become skeptical and believe that the figure is too high. J. C. Russell believes that the mortality rate in England during the two-and-a-half-year period of 1349–51 came to 23.6 percent of the population.[1] Since normal mortality would be 3 percent of the population per year, the plague would have accounted for an excess mortality figure of 16.6 percent. He also estimates that the excess mortality in the one plague-year of 1369 was 10 percent, making the *per annum* rate that year higher than in the earlier era. M. M. Postan on the other hand thinks that 30 percent is the minimum, 40 percent is probable and 50 percent is possible.[2] It is certain however that recurrent plagues and famine provided, during these centuries, the effective check that Malthus described.

Nor did the populations of Northern Europe escape the visitations of death's third messenger – war. The battles of this time, while frequent, did not involve large numbers of men; and did not directly kill a large part of the population. What they did was to destroy the surrounding countryside and in the process of pillaging and looting put the local inhabitants to flight. Whole regions would be periodically depopulated in this way. Organized violence appears to have been endemic in this period: England suffered the War of the Roses and the Great Peasant Revolt, the states of Germany suffered in a similar fashion, and France was bled white by the Hundred Years War and the rising of the Jacquerie. France in particular suffered from the continual presence of war, revolution, pillaging and looting. Famine and pestilence were the legacy of the expansion of population during the preceding century; an expansion that caused the clearing and taking up of marginal lands whose fertility would not support their occupants for an entire lifetime.

This leads us to another question: for how long did the population of Europe decline? We have seen that the decline probably started early in the fourteenth century and certainly by 1350 a sharp drop had occurred. How long did the decline last? Probably as long as the famine and pestilence

[1] See Table 7.2, above.
[2] This figure was given orally by Professor Postan in a conversation at the University of Texas.

continued. Few historians suggest that population had begun its recovery until the last half of the fifteenth century. Recent research using relative prices as the basic information suggests that in England population did not stop falling until 1470 and did not begin to grow rapidly again until the sixteenth century.[3]

While direct observation of the populations of these centuries is impossible, we can observe price movements, both absolute and relative, from evidence that survives. It appears that regional price movements both of products and of the factors of production were everywhere similar in Western Europe. The general price level was characterized during the first three-quarters of the thirteenth century by violent fluctuations, with the peaks seemingly corresponding to famine or plague. Thereafter, the fluctuations in the price level are less pronounced and a slight downward trend becomes apparent. Thus after 1375 deflation characterizes the period: a deflation that appears to last until the sixteenth century. The quantitative evidence from England is the most complete (see Fig. 7.1), but historians have noted the same trend for other areas.

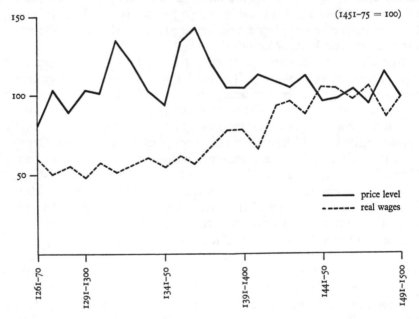

Fig. 7.1. An index of the price level and real wages for England in ten-year averages: 1261–1500.
   Source: Phelps-Brown and Hopkins, 'Seven Centuries of the Prices of Consumables, Compared with Builders' Wage-Rates'.

[3] Clyde G. Reed, 'Price Data and European Economic History' (unpublished PhD dissertation, University of Washington, 1972).

The most important price movements for our purposes are not those of the price level, but the movement of prices relative to each other. Here we observe relative movements opposite to those that occurred during the thirteenth century. Especially important is the fact that the price of agricultural goods fell relative to manufactured goods. In general, a bushel of wheat purchased increasingly less cloth throughout this period. The price of wheat also fell relative to the price of livestock. Here again our evidence is most complete for England, but this tendency also appears to have existed throughout Europe.

Perhaps even more important, the relative prices of the factors of production changed. The price of labor rose relative to that of land. While good evidence exists that the price of labor increased relative to the price level (i.e., that real wages rose), it is more difficult to quantify in detail the rise in the price of labor relative to land rents. Qualitative evidence that this was the case exists in abundance and suggests that it was a universal occurrence throughout Northern Europe.

In sum, there is little doubt that manufactured goods exchanged for more agricultural goods during the fourteenth and fifteenth centuries than they had during the thirteenth; that labor was relatively more expensive both in terms of agricultural and manufactured goods (that is, that a day's labor would now command more of both types of goods); and that the value of labor had risen relative to the value of land. The movements of relative prices during these centuries appears to have been just the opposite of the movement occurring during the thirteenth.

The market, despite the significant decline in population, continued to be an important method for organizing economic activity during the latter Middle Ages. The relative abundance of the price statistics, incomplete as they are, testifies to this. The relative volume of market transactions compared to the allocation of resources by government or voluntary association remains in question. The international trade that had grown so extensively during the thirteenth century survived, but the volume probably declined and its character was altered in the process.

Industrial regions continued to export manufactured products. Flanders and the Low Countries, for instance, continued to export high quality cloth, in return importing foodstuffs. Grain was imported from Germany and France, wool from England and Spain, fish from the North. Throughout Northern Europe, a trade in cloth, wool, wine, foodstuffs, timber, iron and copper continued between regions.

Similarly, the trade between Northern and Southern Europe continued much as it had in the thirteenth century. The nature of trade remained largely unchanged, the staple products of the North being exchanged for the luxury goods and manufactures of the South.

While the basic nature of international trade remained unchanged from the previous century, the volume of trade probably declined. This is a conditional statement because there are no overall trade statistics, and therefore it is not clear that the decline of one city or one area may not have been balanced by the rise of another. Still, the overall implications of the surviving evidence all point to a substantial fall in the volume of trade. Exports of wine from Bordeaux, for example, which were in the neighborhood of 100,000 tons a year in the first decade of the fourteenth century, were down to 13,000 to 14,000 tons in the 1370s. Between 1399 and 1479 exports of wool from Britain fell to two-thirds of their earlier level. However, during this era England was shifting from being an exporter of raw wool to being an exporter of cloth, so it is unclear whether the volume or the composition of trade are reflected in the statistics. The exports of English broadcloth did rise somewhat in the mid-fifteenth century, but fell again until the last quarter of the century when they rose once more. Wine imports into Britain declined. Specific statistics for particular cities such as Marseilles, Genoa and Dieppe all show the same pattern. They show a fall in the volume of trade in the fourteenth and the first half of the fifteenth century, and a resurgence of trade beginning sometime in the last half of the fifteenth century.

Nor do the great Italian city states appear to have been immune from this falling trend. The power and opulence of Venice appears to have continued undiminished for a long period. Yet accounts suggest that the Venetian trade did decline in the fourteenth century and revived in the fifteenth only to begin to wane again after mid-century. The great woolen cloth industry of Florence similarly declined in the fourteenth century. The center of banking, which had shifted from Lombardy to Tuscany, experienced widespread failure in the fourteenth century. The revival of banking led to the Medici family's pre-eminence in the fifteenth century, making Florence the great banking center with branches scattered throughout Europe. In the last half of the fifteenth century Southern Europe was clearly on the decline. The trade in Catalonia, as recorded by Vilar, was only one-fifth of what it had been earlier.

During these tumultous centuries cities in the Low Countries grew. Bruges and Antwerp became the main commercial and financial exchanges for Northern Europe. Merchants native to these places rose to eclipse the itinerant Italians.

II

The major factor in bringing about the end of the expansion characterizing the thirteenth century and in generating the trade depression of the latter Middle Ages was the significant and prolonged decline in population. The immediate effect of the loss of population was an increase in the general price level. Whether this was a real or apparent increase is unclear, since both plague and famine are likely to have appeared, if not simultaneously, at least within the same decade. The influence of plague is to increase the money stock *per capita* as the survivors inherit the wealth of the less fortunate. The effect is to increase the prices of all goods. A famine tends to do the same thing, but also reflects the large relative rise in the price of foodstuffs. The inelastic demand for foodstuffs absorbs both savings and income that in normal years would have been spent on other goods. In short, in famine years the percentage of income spent on foodstuffs increases. The prices of foodstuffs are among the first prices to appear historically. We know what happens to the price of wheat years before we have statistics for the prices of any other goods. It is not clear whether the sharp rise in the prices of foodstuffs reflects an increase in the *per capita* money stock or a dearth of food. In short, our price indexes for the period are too crude for us to be certain of the changes in the level of prices during the fourteenth century.

Assuming that the violent fluctuations of the price index through 1375 reflect a true inflation, thereafter a slow deflation sets in, lasting the rest of the period. One explanation for this deflation suggests that it was linked to the outflow of specie from Northern Europe to the South and eventually to the fabled East. If so, then a persistent decline in the money supply accounts for the deflation. In any event, the surviving evidence is insufficient to refute this explanation.

The decline in population however is sufficient to account for the significant changes in the terms of trade and in relative factor prices. The rise in wages relative to rents was caused by the increased productivity of labor in agriculture as inferior marginal lands were abandoned. As population declined, labor became scarce and hence commanded a higher price in negotiations with landlords, merchants and manufacturers.

While the productivity of labor increased in agriculture, because the new abundance of land allowed only the better land to be cultivated, the productivity of labor in manufacturing remained basically unchanged. This was due to the fact that little land is used in manufacturing. Since the productivity of labor in agriculture was now relatively higher than previously and since its productivity was unchanged in manufacture, the price of manufactures had to rise relative to the price of foodstuffs.

The real wages of labor increased because the productivity of labor overall had gone up and continued to rise as long as population declined. Thus the persons who depended heavily upon their own labor for their livelihood were better off. Generally, those who lived substantially off land rents were significantly worse off. Thus the lot of the peasant, considering only the influence of the decline in population, should have improved while that of his lord worsened.

It would appear from the implicit general equilibrium model employed above that *per capita* income increased throughout the latter Middle Ages, an increase which was accompanied by a significant redistribution of income between the feudal classes. Such an interpretation is perhaps too simple and neat, although its very simplicity is appealing. In order to qualify this optimistic assessment and bring it more into line with the argument of a general recession for the period, it is necessary to consider some factors ignored by the above interpretation.

First it is necessary to explain why the decline in population was so prolonged. A decline in population, lasting more than a century, requires a more complicated explanation than that suggested by a simple Malthusian readjustment. Had this been the case, it could be assumed that once population had initially fallen sufficiently to produce an increase in output *per capita*, population would have stagnated or begun to rise again.

In fact, the explanation is somewhat more complicated. The earlier expansion from the tenth through the thirteenth centuries had, by the end of the era, created a population susceptible to both famine and pestilence. It was the latter which, once it became deeply rooted in the population of Western Europe, remained endemic for a long period, resulting in a continual succession of outbreaks of the plague. These repeated outbreaks of pestilence prevented the recovery of population long after the consequences of relative over-population had disappeared. It appears that not until the medieval populace had acquired a degree of immunity was it able to overcome the plague and to begin to grow again.

The famines and plagues of the period were aided and abetted by a continual succession of military and political struggles. Peasant revolts occurred in almost every European country and workers' risings occurred in the urbanized Low Countries during this period. The repression that generally followed these revolutions added loss of life and physical destruction to the probability of the return of famine and pestilence.

The inhabitants of the era, seemingly favored by higher wages and potentially higher standards of living, were thus also burdened with a highly uncertain future. New taxes were imposed; the loss of property by theft, destruction, or confiscation was possible at any time; and even the loss of life itself was a constant possibility. An uncertain future certainly detracts from the possibility of a higher standard of living. It is not clear therefore whether the potential gains inherent in higher agricultural productivity were realized by the populace during the latter Middle Ages.

The decline of population, coupled with war, confiscation, pillage and revolution, reduced the volume of trade and stimulated a trend toward local self-sufficiency. The losses to society due to the decline in specialization and reduced division of labor certainly argues against a rise in the standard of living. This change was synonymous with increased transaction costs from using the market, a change which increased the incentives for independent groups to rely upon the coercive powers of governments to organize economic activity. It became relatively more profitable to attempt to monopolize trade and manufacture with the aid of government rather than to seek ways of increasing productivity. During the period voluntary groups increasingly combined with government to create institutions which were designed to redistribute income in their favor, all of which reduced the efficiency of the medieval economy. This is in stark contrast to the developments of the previous century when institutional innovations mainly sought to capture productivity gains.

III

The significant and prolonged decline in population induced three parameter shifts which account for the observed changes in the institutional arrangements and the property rights of the period. These changes were: (1) the alteration in relative factor prices with rents falling relatively to the value of labor, and the consequent decline in feudal revenues heavily dependent on land rents; (2) the relative increase in the minimum necessary level of government expenditure; and (3) the rise of the costs (transaction costs) of using the market to organize economic activity. These changes directly affected the nature of institutions and property rights during the latter Middle Ages.

These changed economic conditions required adjustments in the manorial contractual arrangements. The decline in population left the holdings of many peasants and landlords at least partially vacant. The lords initially attempted to force their surviving tenants to take up vacancies on the old customary terms and resisted with such laws as the Statute of Labourers the increase in real wages consistent with the new economic conditions; such attempts quickly came to nought. The flight of peasants, the competition between lords anxious to attract tenants, and the stubborn refusal of villeins to obey orders defeated them.

In Western Europe the most effective way to retain tenants was to lower rents and to relax servile obligations. The latter objective led to the innovation of lengthy leases, which soon came to be life leases, under which labor obligations were combined with customary rents in one fixed rent contract. The inflations of the previous centuries had substantially reduced the real value of the nominal customary fixed rents, so that they provided a close approximation to the current real value of rents and made mutual agreement easy. A life lease was renegotiable only on the death of the tenant – such was the price lords were now willing to pay to obtain tenants. The tenants in effect received the use of the land for life in return for agreed fixed payments to the lord, who still provided the public goods required on the manor.

Life leases turned out to be a last-ditch effort by lords to retain their customary rights by signing them away to only one generation of tenants. But since recurrent plague did not allow the population to expand for several generations, these agreements themselves took on the force of custom and eventually the tenants obtained by customary practice the right of inheritance. In the late fifteenth and sixteenth centuries such arrangements came to be considered as equal in law to copyholds and as subject only to the now customary encumbrance of a fixed money payment or quit rent. A secularly rising price level during the sixteenth century reduced this to a purely nominal payment by the year 1600. The manorial economy thus met its death: labor service were now irrevocably replaced by money rent payments; land was now tilled by free tenants and/or by workers receiving money wages, who were free to seek their best employment.

A second major institutional change during the fourteenth and fifteenth centuries was the rise of the nation-states to rival and eventually eclipse the city states. In the process, the profusion of feudal baronies, local principalities and small kingdoms, which were the hallmark of the high Middle Ages, were consolidated into the nations of England, France, Spain and the Netherlands. We have seen in previous chapters that this process was probably the inevitable result of the development of a money economy and the expansion of trade.

The parameter shifts that most influenced the development of nation-states were the fall in feudal dues stemming from the decline in land rents and the relative rise in the level of expenditures necessary for a government to survive. The former was directly due to the decline in population and the consequent abandonment of extra marginal land. The latter was due in part to the rise in the wages of labor, which substantially increased the cost of any army, and partly to changes in military technology which, to be effectively utilized, required trained and co-ordinated military units rather than a temporary assembly of armored knights.

Thus, at the same time that kings and barons found it necessary to increase their expenditure on a military establishment, they found their revenues from traditional sources declining substantially. These changes dictated fewer military units overall, each of a larger size, than previously, and required a contraction in the number of governmental units, which came about by consolidation, merger and conquest. Whatever the method, this process was apt to prove disruptive to the society. While the consolidation and rise of the nation-state was perhaps inevitable, the process of governmental consolidation in each area was influenced by local conditions and consequently varied between regions.

One of the potential means to increase state revenues was to extend the geographic area of the state's influence and regulation. Conquest was an obvious way to accomplish this and two centuries of warfare was the result. Such an approach was, of course, a zero sum game; what one state won, another lost. Peace between the emerging states was therefore always tenuous; uncertain and unstable at best. Another way was to consolidate the state's power within its existing area of nominal jurisdiction. The several class wars of this era – the revolt of peasants in England, Germany, and Spain and of the Jacquerie in France – provided convincing proof that armies, not knights, were needed to keep the peace internally. A standing army weakened the position of barons relative to that of kings. Finally, merger via marriage, always accompanied by intrigue, and even at times by assassination was a possible method of extending the control of a state.

Another way to increase the income so desperately needed by the emerging nation-states was to seek new sources of revenue. New taxes, loans, and payments for privileges were potential means of obtaining the monies needed. The search for new means was to have important consequences for the development of institutions and property rights during this period. We have suggested above that the decline in the number of independent military units was inevitable, but the means of accomplishing this contraction were diverse. We shall below look briefly at some of the historical variations, but first we should summarize the developments in the art of warfare.

The era opens with the battle of Courtrai in 1302 in which the flower of French knighthood, heavily armoured and mounted, were slaughtered by Flemish burgers using the pike phalanx. It presaged the end of the era of supremacy of heavy cavalry. The dominance of the English longbow during the Hundred Years War, especially at Crecy (1346), Poitiers (1356), and Agincourt (1415), was the despair of the French, who found no effective counter-measure in open battle. The French finally resorted to harrying tactics under Bertrand de Gueselin and the inspiration provided by Joan of Arc. The final battle of the war in 1453 placed entrenched French artillery against English archers and pikemen. The French won; a success that marked the end of the dominance of the longbow. The pike, like the longbow, equally transformed the methods of warfare of these two centuries. If the English longbowmen were the despair of the French, the Swiss pikemen, formed in disciplined ranks, dominated close-in fighting throughout Western Europe and reduced the effectiveness of armored medieval cavalry.

The improvements in the use of weaponry based on gunpowder were slow, but the successful Turkish breach of the walls of Constantinople (1453) indicated that the old-style walled city was becoming obsolete. By the end of the fifteenth century, both the cannon and (less successfully) the handgun were transforming military techniques.

The rise of a money economy not only encouraged the development of specialists – the Genovese crossbowmen, the English longbowmen, the Swiss and German pikemen – but made specialized mercenary units a profitable business. They were, while very effective in battle during the latter Middle Ages, very expensive and dangerous. Dangerous not only to the enemy but also to their employers, when unemployed – and frequently unpaid – the mercenaries preyed on the countryside. Machiavelli deplored their employment but insisted that a successful monarch could not do without them. The alternative, a standing army, had advantages but was still more expensive, since the men had to be paid in both war and peace. Gradually however, standing armies were replacing mercenaries over these centuries. Charles VII of France formed the Compagnies d'Ordonnance in 1445, which eventually was made up of 12,000 troops paid at the rate of 10 livre tournois per month for a man at arms and 4 or 5 livre tournois for each of his 'retinue'.

Taken together, the two centuries show a transformation in warfare and led to an ever-growing fiscal crisis. The financial resources necessary for survival, i.e., to quickly field a modern army, exceeded those available in the traditional feudal barony. The result was an era of almost unbelievable turmoil, amalgamation, terror, murder, internal and external strife, intrigue and counter-intrigue. No short account can explain, much less describe, the machinations involved in the Hundred Years War, the War of the Roses or the internal struggles of Charles VII of France, including those involving his own son, Louis XI. The latter's intricate intrigues with and against his own feudal barons, with the powerful dukes of Burgundy, and his eventual triumph defy short descriptions. Nor were these tumultous times any different amongst the German states, Spain, Portugal or the Italian states. The result was, however, perfectly clear. Whether by marriage, purchase, perfidy, intrigue or military conquest, the nation-state replaced the feudal barony as the seat of coercive power by the end of the period. The grip that each monarch had upon his subjects, however, differed drastically from one nation to another.

With the advent of the Hundred Years War the French fiscal problems of the fourteenth century required desperate improvisation. With English invasion a reality and no easy export trade to tax, Charles V by 1370 succeeded in imposing a direct tax, the *Taille*, payable by non-nobles (with the clergy also exempted). Together with *Aides* (a sales tax) and the *Gabelle* (a monopoly of the salt trade), they were the new sources of French revenue – initially considered to be extraordinary. By the middle of Charles VII's reign, they were permanent taxes and exceeded the traditional 'feudal' revenues thirty-three-fold. In fact, the revenue from the *Taille* grew from 1.2 million livre tournois in Charles VII's reign in the mid-fifteenth century, to 4.6 million livre tournois in 1481. Unlike their

English counterpart, the French national and regional representative bodies relinquished control over the *Taille*.[4] The nobility and clergy that made up these assemblies were personally exempted and some of them had acquired a vested interest in the tax. They were in charge of collecting the tax in their locality and, frequently were permitted to retain a share; or else the pensions they exacted from the Crown were paid out of the tax. The consequence of the Estates General's loss of the power to tax was significant. The French representative bodies in effect withered away and by the end of Louis XI's reign they provided no political checks upon the king's activity. The term 'absolute ruler' often applied to French kings, however, is misleading, since a ruler must always take into account the possibility of external conquest or of revolt by his subjects. But the degrees of freedom which the French monarch achieved were striking in contrast to his English counterpart. These differences would have a major influence on the subsequent economic development of the two countries.

In England the receipts from traditional feudal revenues were, as in France, a declining portion of total state revenues. The lay subsidy and the clerical subsidy (in effect a form of property taxation) were granted respectively by parliament and by church convocations. However, it was England's external trade which provided the bulk of the increased Crown revenue. Taxes on wine imports, general merchandise and wool cloth were sources of income. The main source, however, in the thirteenth century was the wool trade. The wool tax formed the backbone of the augmented Crown revenue. This custom alone yielded £30,000 a year by the later fifteenth century.

The story of the way the three groups involved in the wool trade (the exporters, the wool growers as represented in parliament, and the Crown) arrived at an agreement has been expertly told by Eileen Power.[5] In this agreement, the merchants of the staple achieved a monopoly of the export trade and a depot in Calais, parliament received the right to set the tax, and the Crown obtained the revenue. In contrast to France, the burden of taxation fell on groups with some political power: the landlords and the merchants. In England from the Magna Carta on, we observe that the Crown was forced to trade privileges for *revenue*. The whole process is well described by Stubbs.

> The admission of the right of parliament to legislate, to inquire into abuses, and to share in the guidance of national policy, was practically purchased by the money granted to Edward I and Edward III; although Edward I had a just theory of national unity, and Edward III exercised little more political foresight than prompted him to seek the acquiescence

[4] We discuss the history of French fiscal policy in more detail in Chapter 10 below.
[5] Eileen Power, *The Wool Trade In English Medieval History* (Clarendon Press, 1941).

of the nation in his own schemes. It had been well said that although the English people have never been slow to shed their blood in defence of liberty, most of the limitations by which at different times they have succeeded in binding the royal power have been purchased with money; many of them by stipulated payments in the offering and accepting of which neither party saw anything to be ashamed of. The confirmation of the charters in 1225 by Henry III contains a straight-forward admission of the fact, 'for this concession and for the gift of these liberties and those contained in the charter of the forests, the archbishops, bishops, abbots, priors, earls, barons, knights, freeholders and all men of the realm granted us a fifteenth part of all their moveable goods'.

The charter of the national liberties was in fact drawn up just like the charter of a privileged town. In 1297 Edward I in equally plain terms recognized the price which he had taken for renewal of the charter of his father. In 1301 at Lincoln, the barons on behalf of the whole community told the king that if their demands were granted they would increase their gift from a tenth to a fifteenth; in 1310 they told Edward II that they had by the gift of a twentieth purchased relief from prises and other grievances; in 1339 the king informed the commons, by way of inducing them to be liberal, that the chancellor was empowered to grant some favours to the nation in general, 'as grantz et as petitz de la commune'; to which they replied in the next session that if their conditions were not fulfilled they would not be bound to grant the aid. The rehearsal, in the statutes of 1340 and later years, of the conditions on which the money grants of those years were bestowed, shows that the idea was familiar. It furnished in fact a practical solution of difficult questions which in theory were insoluble. The king had rights as lord of his people, the people had rights as freemen and as the estates of the realm which the king personified; the definition of the rights of each, in theory most difficult, became practically easy when it was reduced to a question of bargain and sale.[6]

The relationship between the state and the private sector in the Netherlands represents a story too complicated to relate in detail here. The conflict between feudal and national interests during these strife-torn years was complicated in the Low Countries by the internal strife between the artisans and patricians within the basically autonomous individual towns. Yet the great export trade of the Low Countries in wool cloth and metal products made the whole region a rich prize. When the Burgundians acquired the area they set about increasing their fiscal revenues by encouraging trade and commerce. Under Philip the Good, Antwerp became the great commercial

[6] William Stubbs, *The Constitutional History of England* (Clarendon Press, 1896), vol. 2, pp. 599–601.

center of Europe. He established a uniform coinage system in 1433. The cloth industry, hidebound by town guild restrictions, was encouraged to move to the free environment of the countryside. The shipping and fishing industry prospered, like the cloth industry, at the expense of the guild-ridden Hanse. Again, however, it is in the political structure that the implications for long-run efficient property rights are found. The Burgundian system is succinctly described in the following paragraph.

> The Dukes created a set of central institutions, which amounted to federation. The Great Council, in which all the provinces were represented, little by little imposed its authority over all matters outside the local constitutions. Its judicial section became in 1473 the Parlement of Malines, the supreme court of appeal. In 1471, a standing army was created in the *Compagnies d'Ordonnance*. Most important was the summons (1463) by Philip the Good of the Estates General, consisting of the representatives of the provincial Estates. Taxes could only be levied by consent of the local assemblies, and the Estates General were in fact a congress of them. The new federal monarchy remained limited in spite of the absolutist tendencies of its dukes, a common feature of the century. In short, with freedom of individual enterprise, with the organization of internal peace and justice and finance within a wide territory of a national character, the Netherlands were going through the slow and chequered evolution from late medieval to modern times.[7]

The evolution of a nation-state in Spain was characterized by a now-familiar pattern of internal chaos and external aggression. In the case of Spain it was complicated by the existing Moorish states which were not finally defeated until the capture of Grenada in 1492. Before Castile came to dominate Spain there were diverse patterns of political structure in evidence, but it is worth noting that the Cortes of Catalonia exerted an influence over the royal purse strings similar to the English parliament and retained some degree of fiscal autonomy throughout the whole period. While the central story of Spanish development is with Castile, it is noteworthy that Catalonia enjoyed far greater economic development than the rest of Spain. The Cortes there enjoyed some influence in the thirteenth century and the nobles, exempt from the major land taxes, managed to share in the revenues. The early taxes, such as the alcabala, a sales tax, and the sisa, a turnover tax, were imposed on top of municipal and local levies. However, it was the revenues from the Mesta which provided the major and fastest-growing source of the Crown's fiscal revenue.

While land was still abundant, the wool industry developed and sheep-herding between the highlands in summer and the lowlands in winter

[7] *The Shorter Cambridge Medieval History* (Cambridge University Press, 1952), vol. 2, pp. 1044–5.

became the pattern. Local shepherds' guilds called *mestas* were consolidated by Alfonso X in 1723 into a single guild called the Honorable Assembly of the Mesta of the Shepherds of Castile.

The motive was merely one of the king's financial embarrassment; he realized that it was much easier to assess taxes on livestock than on men, and formed the mestas into an organization that would provide considerable sums to the monarchy. In exchange for these taxes the herders wrested a series of privileges from Alfonso X, the most important of which was the extension of supervision over all migratory flocks, including stray animals, in the whole kingdom of Castile. This supervisory function was gradually extended, in time, even to 'permanent' sheep pastured in local mestas and to the 'riberiegas', animals which were pastured along the river banks within the district of a particular town.[8]

It was under Ferdinand and Isabella that a nation-state emerged from internal strife and that power became centralized in the monarchy at the expense of the local lords. The revenues of the state grew as a consequence from 800,000 marovedis in 1470 to 22 million marovedis in 1504. Yet the union was more political than economic, since the Catalans were excluded from economic participation by various specific rules. Isabella's and Ferdinand's success, as elsewhere, came from a populace weary of the terroristic internal strife of nobles and willing to have an end even at the expense of loss of representation. After 1480, the Cortes of Castile is rarely summoned and an 'orderly despotism' succeeded.

Thus nation-states evolved in the Netherlands, England, France and Spain. The nature of the state differed between regions. France and Spain developed 'absolute' monarchies, while the Netherlands and England succeeded in placing checks upon their rulers in the form of representative assemblies. The nature of the state and the different limitations faced by the monarchs of each were to influence, as we shall see, the character of its institutions and property rights.

IV

The fourteenth century begins with the advent of Malthusian-type checks to continued population growth. The population of Western Europe fell throughout the century and remained at a reduced level for perhaps a century and a half. The reduction in population reversed the relative factor scarcities that had prevailed during the previous century. This influenced the economic organization of society, reversing to some extent the changes that had taken place during the thirteenth century. A complete reversal to

---

[8] Jaime Vicens Vives, *An Economic History of Spain* (Princeton University Press, 1969), p. 25.

the relatively self-sufficient manorial–feudal economy of the tenth century did not occur. A money economy, for instance, persisted, as did many of the customs that had evolved over the previous few centuries.

The institutional structure of the feudal world had irrevocably been replaced by the nation-state. In effect, the mix between voluntary institutional arrangements, markets and government had been basically altered. A money economy and technological changes had increased the scale of warfare and, in consequence, the size of governmental units. Anarchy, chaos and shrinking population had raised transactions costs in many areas, thereby increasing the size of both governmental units and voluntary organizations at the expense of the market. In agriculture there were conflicting forces at work. The disintegration of the manor led to an increasing use of the market at the same time that the rising transactions costs cited above led to some reversion to self-sufficiency.

The most striking development was the emergence of the nation-state. Born in expanding warfare, created by intrigue and treachery, the crowned heads appeared to have more the characteristics of Mafia bosses than the characteristics of kings envisioned a century later by John Locke. The 'absolutism' of Louis XI in matters of taxation led to a substantial rise in royal revenue. Yet what set limits on his revenues? In common with every other crowned head of Europe, the king of France was usually desperately short of revenues. Clearly the constraints were very real and reflected the likelihood of revolt or the emigration of his subjects. Yet the Mafia analogy has an important element of truth. The citizens were buying protection and were willing to pay for it. The incessant baronial warfare, the pillaging by mercenary bands roaming the countryside and the possibility of foreign invasion threatened the citizenry. A king who credibly offered protection – even a despot – was far preferable to the chaotic conditions which prevailed. While the security of existing property rights was still tenuous under a despot, it was far less tenuous than under anarchy. The most striking feature was the differing structure of the monarchs control over the state purse-strings. In England and the Low Countries, representative bodies set the taxes and the king traded privileges (property rights) and policy for more revenue. In France and Spain, the Estates General and Cortes gradually lost power. The explanation advanced in this chapter is surely tentative, but turns on the sources of potential revenue, the incidence of these revenue sources and the political power of those who bore the tax burden.

The state had taken over from the manor and local baron the majority of the functions of providing justice and protection (although the variations described above should be noted).

The increase in the real value of labor which continued throughout the period had enabled the serf to bargain his way to something that approximated free labor, just as the lord was gradually being transformed into a modern landlord. In the agricultural world, therefore, we see a gradual transformation from an institutional arrangement outside the market to one involving market relationships; rents and wages and the family farm replaced the manorial structure. Yet there were some reversions to self-sufficiency in agriculture, where persistent anarchy or reduced population (and in consequence higher transactions costs) made the market a more expensive way of allocating resources than it had been in the thirteenth century.

In the non-agricultural sector, the later Middle Ages brought a century or more of shrinking markets. It is true that there were exceptions; the Italian cities appeared less affected and Genoa even grew at the expense of rivals. In general, however, there was a decline of market towns and fierce competition for existing interregional and international trade. The Hanseatic League, which developed as a collusive arrangement to protect its existing markets, was gradually displaced by Low Country competition. The most striking feature was the growing power of guilds, whether agricultural (the Mesta), multi-city (the Hanse), or the individual artisan guilds in the towns. The fundamental objective of the guild in this era of fierce competition for shrinking markets was to develop a degree of monopoly power and, consequently, to limit supply. The result was a higher product price and lower output than would have occurred in the absence of the guilds. In effect the consequence was a shift away from the market to an institutional arrangement that used the market less than more competitive organizational arrangements.

The key to monopoly power was the coercive power to limit entry into the market. A most important characteristic of those two centuries was the shift in the locus of coercive power from private policing or local baronial protection to the nation-state. Just as justice and protection shifted out of the hands of the barons to those of the king, so did the sanctioning and protection of guild monopolies. The king, by the end of the Middle Ages, was in a position to enforce exclusive rights to markets within his kingdom. Voluntary associations of artisans and merchants organized in guilds were willing to pay for the exclusive privileges that only the king could now provide.

It is hard to escape the conclusion that these were indeed dismal centuries, with famine, plague, persistent warfare and, in the periods between wars, roaming bands of unemployed mercenaries looting the countryside. It was the end of an era; the disintegration of the traditional form of societal organization and the birth – painful and prolonged – of a new order.

Did living standards rise or fall? There can be no doubt that the more favorable land/man ratio up to 1450 led to rising real wages for agricultural laborers. On the other hand, falling rents reduced the income of the rentier.

On balance, these two changes alone would have led to rising *per capita* income. But when we add the consequences of decreasing market size, anarchy, and the consequent rising transactions costs the overall results are far less clear.

It is appropriate that we end this chapter on a more positive note. Not only was the nation-state an improvement (in most people's minds) over baronial anarchy, but in the last half of the fifteenth century we begin to see again a growing population. The revival of markets followed apace and man's quest for commerce extended beyond the bounds of continental Europe. The explorations encouraged by Prince Henry the Navigator of Portugal were made possible by the revival of commerce and by improvements in ships and navigation. By the end of the century they had opened up not only new commercial sources but a new world for colonization.

8. FISCAL POLICY AND PROPERTY RIGHTS

We established in Chapter 1 that an efficient economic organization is the basic requirement for economic growth. If such an organization exists then a society will grow if it so desires. Ideally, by providing the proper incentives, a fully efficient economic organization would insure that the private and social rates of return were the same for each activity and that both were equal among all economic activities. Such a situation would require that each individual desires to maximize his wealth and that he has the exclusive right to use as he sees fit his land, labor, capital, and other possessions; also that he alone has the right to transfer his resources to another, and that property rights are so defined that no one else is either benefited or harmed by his use of his property.

If such an economic Shangri-La were to be instituted for the society as a whole, the proper amount of research and development would be performed, new knowledge would be applied to economic activities at the proper time, the correct amount of human and physical capital would be available and utilized, and each factor of production would receive the value of its contribution at the margin to output. In sum, the society would grow at the optimal rate determined by its preference for current goods relative to future goods.

Not even in modern times have these conditions existed, for the transaction costs of establishing such an economic organization would be prohibitive. While property rights remain imperfectly defined or enforced, private and social returns in some activities continue to diverge because some of the costs or benefits due an individual who uses or transfers his resources will accrue instead to a third party. This discrepancy persists because, given the existing political and economic organization of the economy, the costs of eliminating each externality would exceed the benefits. In any specific situation, it might be too expensive to negotiate a contractual arrangement with every person affected by an economic activity, or it might be impossible to measure efficiently the external costs or benefits imposed or to influence the government to change the situation. Thus the correction hinges on both contractual and measurement costs, and where either sort is present the externality will persist until changes in the economic world increase the benefits relative to the costs of internalizing it.

I

We have seen that to some extent such a change in relative values was brought about by a growing population during the Middle Ages. As a result, strides were made towards improving the economic organization of Western Europe. The lord–serf relationship, for instance, slowly yielded to a relationship between landowner–occupier (or landowner–tenant) and wage-earners. With equal deliberation, the unwritten 'customary' law gave way to an ever-increasing extent to a body of written law which explicitly defined personal rights and property as the myriad surviving customary rights became incorporated and consolidated. Especially in the factor markets conditions were improved. Labor was now generally free to seek its best rewards and keep most of what was earned, and land came to be regarded as property which could be transferred.

However, capital markets and the organization of commerce were still burdened by usury laws and by the ethical concept of a 'just' price, which could be circumvented only by more expensive alternative arrangements. Product markets, especially for manufacturers, were often monopolized and outsiders prevented from entering the trade. Few inducements encouraged investment in research or development. Even as private property rights came into existence, their enforcement remained uncertain and subject to the vagaries of the political situation generated by the emergence of nation-states. The very process of economic and political change was associated with additional costs of uncertainty about what the future arrangements would be.

To continue our summation of changing medieval conditions brought about by population growth, we recall that as the market expanded, efficiency required the substitution of money payments for labor dues in a new contractual arrangement. In the process serfdom died, labor became free to seek its best rewards, land received rent, and the basic feudal-manorial relationship withered and died. Also, thanks to a market economy, governments could now receive taxes in the form of money instead of labor services, and were thereby enabled to hire their own specialized bureaucracies and armies as needed.

In general, with the exception of the capital market, the improvement in the organization of the factor markets during the Middle Ages proceeded ahead of that of the product markets. The product markets outside the international fairs were plagued with imperfections in the form of privileged guilds and monopolies. The gains made in extending the market economy throughout Europe occurred despite these handicaps.

II

The greatest gains that could be achieved during the early modern period were in improving the efficiency with which goods could be exchanged. Production for the market involves besides the production of the good the process of making various transfers until the good reaches the consumer. Improvements in the methods of producing both agricultural and manufactured products were hindered by the absence of property rights protecting new techniques. Thus technological change during this era, when it occurred, was, as during the Middle Ages, generally the result of specialization due to the extension of the market. The production of agricultural products on the one hand, due to the fixed amount of land, was subject to diminishing returns, while on the other hand manufacturing, not so burdened, exhibited constant returns to scale.

Besides the resources used in directly producing goods are resources used in transferring these goods. The transfer of goods between economic units requires the provision of information about the opportunities for exchange or *search costs*, the negotiation of the terms of the exchange– *negotiation costs* – and determining procedures for enforcing the contract– *enforcement costs*. The costs of providing all the services involved are called here *transaction costs*.

The economy's demand for the services of the transaction sector is derived from the demand for the products exchanged – one goes with the other. The market demand for goods is a function of the potential gains from trade, which depend, as we have seen above, upon the preferences of individuals and upon the resource endowments between regions. The growth in population, where it occurred, during the early modern period, continued to expand the potential gains from trade throughout Western Europe as it had during the Middle Ages.

Where the potential gains from trade expanded so did the demand for transactions. The transactions sector, unlike the production of industrial or agricultural goods, is subject to economies of scale. That is, as the output of the sector increases, the unit cost of trades declines. Economies of scale depend upon a cost function with a fixed component. As the output of the sector increases, the unit cost of the fixed component declines. Thus an expanding market economy can increase the *per capita* income of its inhabitants, in the absence of technological change, if the gains due to economies of scale in transactions outweigh the losses due to declining productivity in agriculture.

Certain fixed costs are involved in each of the three categories of transaction costs. Search costs, for example, involve a fixed expense in gathering market information. Once information is gathered any number of potential buyers and sellers could use the information. The cost of gathering the information is not influenced by the number of persons using it. So the larger the number the lower the unit cost. The cost of disseminating market information is probably proportional with distance, but centralization of buyers and sellers in one market also reduces the unit cost. Negotiation costs at any point in time are probably variable but as the scale of transactions increases, it becomes profitable to institute standard practices or basic trade terms from which to begin negotiations. Thus not all clauses in an agreement must be haggled over. Enforcement costs are also subject to economies of scale, in that a fixed cost is involved in establishing procedures and laws, and in influencing the government. Thus as the scale of transactions increases, the unit cost of using the market declines.

Given the improvements in the factor markets that had occurred in the Middle Ages, major gains remained to be made in the transactions sector and in the closely related capital market. The absence until the end of this period of an effective means of stimulating invention served as a brake upon developing new productive techniques. However the knowledge necessary to increase the efficiency of the market was already known, having been developed earlier by the Italians. All that remained was to adapt these improvements as the scale of transactions warranted.

III

The countries that altered their fundamental institutional arrangements to exploit these opportunities grew, but it was not inevitable that this would occur. For as trade was expanding a need was created for larger political units to define, protect, and enforce property rights over greater areas (thus internalizing some of the costs of long-distance commerce). The provision of governmental services was also subject over some range of output to economies of scale. A set of property rights once specified can be extended almost indefinitely to other areas at little additional cost. For example a court system to adjudicate disputes and to enforce law is more efficient the more specialized it is. The ability to hire mercenaries as needed or to maintain a standing army permitted the more efficient provision of protection to a larger area.

Between the thirteenth and fifteenth centuries there was also a series of major technological changes in military warfare, of which the longbow, the pike and gunpowder (and in consequence the cannon and the musket) were the most important. Whether the development of an exchange economy was a sufficient condition for expanding the optimum scale of warfare or whether it was augmented by the aforementioned innovations is not clear. However, the overall consequence was that the conditions for political survival were drastically altered and entailed not only larger numbers for an army of an effective size, but also much more training and discipline (particularly important for effective pikemen) and much more costly equipment in the form of cannons and muskets. The age of the armoured knight with lance, and the era of chivalry was passed. Instead it was the age of the Genovese crossbowman, the English (or Welsh) longbowmen and the Swiss pikemen, all for hire to the highest bidder.

As the demands of a growing market economy thus imposed pressure to establish larger units of government, the multitude of local manors faced the choice of enlarging their own jurisdictions over neighboring manors, combining with other manors to do so, or of surrendering certain of their traditional political prerogatives. Beginning with the rise of the market, throughout Western Europe more and more of the functions of government were assumed by regional and national political units in a growing ground-swell leading eventually toward the creation of nation-states.

At this point we can usefully pause in our historical narrative to offer an analogy from economic theory. Take the case of a competitive industry with a large number of small firms. Introduce an innovation which leads to economies of scale over a substantial range of output so that the efficient size for a firm is much larger. The path from the old competitive equilibrium to a new (and probably unstable) oligopoly solution will be as follows. The original small firms must either increase in size, combine, or be forced into bankruptcy. The result is a small number of large firms of optimum size, but even then the results are unstable. There are endless efforts toward collusion and price fixing, but equally ubiquitous are the advantages that will accrue to an individual firm which cheats on the arrangement. The result is periods of truce interrupted by eras of cut-throat competition.

When we translate the above description to the political world of this era we have an exact analogy. Between 1200 and 1500 the many political units of Western Europe went through endless expansions, alliances and combinations in a world of continual intrigue and warfare. Even as the major nation-states emerged, the periods of peace were continually inter-rupted. In short it was an era of expanding war, diplomacy and intrigue. The magnitude of the increasing cost was staggering. A year of warfare represented at least a fourfold increase in costs of government – and most years were characterized by war, not peace. Monarchs were continuously beset by immense indebtedness and forced to desperate expedients; the specter of bankruptcy was a recurring threat and for many states a reality. The fact of the matter is that princes were not free – they were bound to an unending runaway fiscal crisis.

This process was neither smooth nor painless. Each growing political unit encountered not only harassing fiscal problems, but inevitable com-petition with ambitious rivals, which involved endless political alliances, combinations, intrigues, and even warfare. The cost of consolidation and expansion by any of these routes was enormously high by the scale of traditional feudal revenues.

The situation was aggravated by the decline in population in the fourteenth century and its failure to recover during the next. The struggling infant regional and national states of the fourteenth and fifteenth centuries found that the use of trained and disciplined professional soldiers had increased the optimal size of an army and that each soldier individually cost more, due to the relative increase in wages resulting from population decline. For the same reason, the money value of feudal obligations often based upon land rents declined. Facing continual financial crises, the embryonic competing nation-states soon found that survival demanded ever larger revenues which could come only from new sources. Those political units which were relatively more efficient at solving their fiscal problems survived; the relatively inefficient were absorbed by their rivals.

In the face of declining revenues and growing financial needs, the princes of Europe faced an ever growing dilemma. Custom and tradition set limits to the exactions they could obtain from lesser lords and as the Magna Carta amply attests, a king who stepped over the boundary of accepted custom faced the ever-present possibility of revolt. Many of the king's vassals were almost as powerful as he (in fact the dukes of Burgundy were much more powerful than the kings of France) and certainly in concert they were more powerful. There was frequently more than one active contender for the throne, but even in the absence of an active contender powerful vassals posed a continuous imminent threat either to overthrow the king from within or to collaborate with outside invasion threats (as the Burgundians did with England against the French crown). There was the possibility of borrowing the money, as indeed a long succession of first Italian and then German bankers could attest, and this was an important way of meeting the short-term crisis of a war. However, a prince could not be sued and accordingly the lender exacted a high interest rate (usually disguised to avoid usury laws) for the high risk, or collateral (early it was crown lands, then crown jewels, or farming the customs or monopoly concessions). Still default was common. Edward III ruined the Peruzzi and Bardi and at a later date Charles V and Phillip II ruined the Genovese and the Fuggers. The capital market for princes was not only one of the most thriving activities of this period, but a major force in the development of the financial centers of Florence, Antwerp and Amsterdam.

Yet loans, if they were to be repaid required fiscal revenues. Loans could tide a king through a war but then he faced the awesome task of repayment. If lending to princes was a major influence in the development of capital markets, the development of a regular source of revenue to repay the loans was the guiding influence in the relationships between the state and the private sector.

While it was certain that larger political units would eventually evolve, the question became: which of the many small states could prove their right to continued existence by exhibiting relative efficiency? Each state, involved in a fight for survival, desperately sought new sources of fiscal revenues. Confiscation offered a short-run solution, but would likely prove costly if not fatal in the longer run. Alternatively, the state could offer, for a price, to benefit the private sector by redefining or altering property rights, or by more efficiently enforcing those already on the books. Charges could be levied for the state's permission to exploit profitable opportunities newly discovered or made feasible by an expanding or contracting market.

Since these favors were certain to go to the highest bidder, there was no assurance that these institutional changes would be more efficient from society's point of view; given the state of property rights in 1500, the private rate of return on most activities was apt to be substantially different from the social rate. Here, exactly, is a crucial point in our argument: the differences in the performance of the economies of Western Europe between 1500 and 1700 was in the main due to the type of property rights created by the emerging states in response to their continuing fiscal crisis. Let us see why this was so.

IV

To understand the background, we must explain the functions of the state against a wider background than would be necessary in dealing with the feudal world alone. Even in our day, the government is primarily an institutional arrangement that sells protection and justice to its constituents. It does so by monopolizing the definition and enforcement of property rights over goods and resources and the granting of rights to the transfer of these assets. In return for this service, the state receives payment in the form of taxes. Since economies of scale in the provision of protection and justice make this transaction potentially worthwhile to the constituents, a basis exists for a mutually advantageous trade between the governed and the government. So long as economies of scale continue, the state's widened protection and enforcement of property rights increases the income of all constituents and this saving is divided in some manner between the constituents and the state.

What determines the division of these savings? The citizens are interested in receiving as much of the incremental income as possible; but so is the state, since its very survival during this period often depends on the maximization of present revenues. Let us consider again the historical evidence of the fourteenth and fifteenth centuries as described in Chapter 7.

In those two troubled centuries we have seen that more than one potential supplier was eager to provide governmental services to an area in return for revenues. Numerous powerful vassals of a king within any political unit were quite ready to assume control. Equally, outsiders, in the form of rival kings or dukes of other political units, were always poised, ready to take over. The constituents logically would accept that 'state' which offered them the greatest percentage of the gains from the wider administration of protection and justice. In fact the 'ideal' solution for the constituents was one in which they were delegated the 'constitutional' power to set the price (tax), whereas the opposite was true from the viewpoint of the monarch, whose security rested on the degree to which the Crown had a free hand in determining the source and the rate of taxation. The more monopoly power an existing prince could claim – that is, the less close or threatening were his rivals – the greater the percentage of rents which the state could appropriate.

We have already indicated the reasons for the different patterns which were emerging in England and France. In the former, parliament had been able to wrest control over taxing power from the monarch. In the latter, the chaos of the fifteenth century, in which all property rights were insecure, had led the Estates General to give up power over taxes to Charles VII in return for a promise of increased order and protection against marauding bands of mercenaries and English invaders. In the process of keeping his promise, the French king eliminated his close rivals, placing the Crown in a better position to demand a larger share of the social savings generated by government.

The structure of the economy must always determine which sectors of the economy can most profitably be taxed by the state.

The net benefits to the state of altering and protecting property rights in any sector will be determined not only by the social benefits, but also by the transaction costs involved. The gains available to the state from devising new property rights depend upon the actual benefits or savings created, minus the costs of creating the new institutional arrangement. The cost of negotiating and devising the new arrangements, of measuring the benefits, collecting the appropriate taxes and enforcing the new property rights must be subtracted from society's saving to obtain the revenues directly gained by the state. Each young nation-state under the urgent stresses and strains of the early modern period was most interested in devising new arrangements that maximized its immediate income. It is a foregone conclusion that, given the urgent pressures, the new institutional arrangements created were often not those that maximized society's gain.

The government, for example, could just as easily continue to grant and/or protect inefficient property rights (such as monopolies and guilds) as create more efficient rights, guaranteeing, for instance, open markets. The beneficiaries of a monopoly were easily identified, the private benefits measured and the tax readily negotiated. Enforcement of the monopoly by the state was not difficult, since the monopolist could inform the authorities of violations and the collection of the tax was easy. The granting of privileges was a potentially lucrative and relatively inexpensive source of revenue for the state. The creation of an open market, on the other hand, involves great difficulty in identifying and negotiating with the beneficiaries and the uncertainties and difficulties in establishing and collecting a tax are manifold. However, if, because of limitations faced by the state, the creation and enforcement of this type of property right proves the most profitable source of revenue, then it will be created.

The degrees of freedom available to a prince in his search for revenues varied widely throughout Europe. He could confiscate wealth, but that was a once and for all source of revenue. He could exact a forced loan when his subjects could be convinced that they were threatened by attack or invasion. He could trade the granting of privileges for revenue. These privileges essentially consisted of the granting of property rights or a guarantee of the protection of property rights for revenue. Clearly there were economies of scale in the state taking over from voluntary associations the protection of property rights. As trade and commerce grew beyond the boundaries of the manor and the town, the farmers, merchants and shippers found that the private costs of protection could be reduced by a larger coercive authority. The basis for a mutually advantageous exchange between the government and the governed existed, but no two monarchs were confronted with identical economies. Since individuals in the private sector always had the 'free rider' incentive to evade the tax, the monarch had to discover a source of income that was measurable and easy to collect. In contrast to present-day tax structures, there was no institutional structure available to undertake such activities and as a result in most cases the information costs were so high that they precluded modern alternatives. Two extremes illustrate the dilemma and the possibilities open to the struggling state. (1) Where foreign trade was a significant part of the economy, the costs of measurement and of collection of taxes were typically low – even lower in the case of waterborn trade, since the number of ports was limited. (2) Where trade was primarily local within a town or small geographic area or primarily internal to the economy, the costs of measurement and collection of taxes on trade were typically much higher.

In the former case a tax on imports or exports was probably the most efficient tax to levy from the point of view of the state. In the latter case, the grant of monopolies or taxes upon the factors of production might be most efficient. In any event the nature of the tax and the way in which it was imposed and collected were crucial to economic efficiency.

In the space of this chapter we can no more than list some of the multitudinous (and ingenious) ways by which princes traded property rights for revenue. The right to alienate land was granted in England by the Statute of *Quia emptores* in 1290 (and 1327 for nobles), because the king would otherwise lose revenue by subinfeudation; still later the Statute of Wills (1540) was enacted to permit inheritance because he was losing revenue through the extensive devise of 'uses'. Similar developments were undertaken in France, Champagne and Anjou, not only to prevent loss of revenue but to tax land transfers in the thirteenth century. Towns were granted trading and monopoly privileges in return for revenue, alien merchants were granted legal rights and exemption from guild restrictions in return for revenue. Guilds were granted exclusive monopoly privileges in return for payment to the Crown; custom duties were established on exports and imports in return for monopoly privileges. In some cases the Crown was forced to grant 'representative' bodies control over tax rates in return for the revenue.

This last point requires special emphasis and further elaboration, since it is the key to the differential patterns of development which we observe after 1500. What did the prince have to give up in order to get the essential tax revenues for survival, i.e., what determined his bargaining strength *vis-à-vis* his 'constituents'. The argument advanced above suggests three basic considerations: (1) the incremental gains to constituents from the state taking over the protection of property rights from voluntary associations; (2) the closeness of competitors able to provide the same service; (3) and the structure of the economy which determined the benefits and costs to the Crown of alternative forms of taxation.

V

We can now return to the central issue. The combination of variables described above in no way assured that any emergent state would establish a set of property rights designed to encourage long-run economic growth. During this era the greatest gains were to be made in encouraging the transactions sector. The fiscal needs of the government, however, were always paramount and a monarch could seldom, if ever, afford the luxury of contemplating the consequences of reform and revenues several years hence. Survival was at stake. Given such a foreshortened time horizon, it is not at all surprising that maximization of the present value of state income frequently led to the formation of property rights which actually throttled economic expansion. On the other hand, a different combination of factors might, perhaps accidentally, lead to property rights more conducive to long-term growth being established.

In this last section, we shall examine the differential performance of the economies of Western Europe (given the limits of available evidence) and then, using the framework developed above, trace the emergence of the contrasting sets of property rights that on the one hand produced sustained growth in the Netherlands and in England and on the other led to relative retardation in the case of France and to stagnation and decline in the instance of Spain.

9. THE EARLY MODERN PERIOD

The year 1500 is widely recognized by historians as the watershed between the medieval world and the modern world. The first two centuries of this newer epoch contained much of historical importance, spanning such widely varied events as a price revolution, a commercial revolution, a reformation, a renaissance, voyages of discovery, the colonization of the New World, the development of world trade and the emergence of national states as the dominant form of political organization in Europe.

The nature of historical scholarship in part explains the deplorable lack of any consistent explanation for the momentous occurrences in these two crucial centuries. Most professional historians share a fashionable tendency to spurn generalizations, preferring to devote highly specialized attention to one area during one period of time. Thus few professional scholars have ever attempted a systematically cosmic look at so large a topic as Europe during the sixteenth and seventeenth centuries.

One significant exception to this last statement and possibly to the preceding ones is provided by the Marxist historians, whose theory of history runs into trouble with these two centuries. According to their credo, feudalism is succeeded by capitalism. The problem is that feudalism in Western Europe was buried by 1500, but capitalism as it is known today was not yet born and the industrial revolution was fully two-and-a-half centuries into the future. Thus 'nascent capitalism' or 'commercial capitalism' has been invented to fill this time span, as a stage of economic organization complete with Marxian dynamics – a period of expansion during the sixteenth century and a crisis (contraction) during the seventeenth century, which led into capitalism and the industrial revolution. No such problem of hiatus exists for our explanation. Sometime in the fifteenth century a new Malthusian cycle began. New growth in population made up the losses of the fourteenth century, until eventually diminishing returns were again encountered. Many of the economic factors of the thirteenth century were apparently repeated during the sixteenth, and some of the problems of the fourteenth century recurred during the seventeenth. This time, however, a new phenomenon happened: although in the sixteenth century population was growing all over Europe, the subsequent 'crisis', which might have been expected to be equally ubiquitous, was, in fact, geographically spotty. Some areas and nations proved able to adjust and even to continue to grow, both extensively and intensively, while others emulated the general contraction of the fourteenth century and declined.

The closing years of the seventeenth century revealed winners like Holland and England, 'also rans' like France, and clear losers such as Spain, Italy and Germany. For the first time in history, some regions and nations had been able to escape the iron teeth of the Malthusian trap, while others had failed. What made the crucial difference?

I

Let us briefly examine the overall economic performance of the economies of Western Europe during these two centuries. When the population of Europe began to recover from the Malthusian checks of the fourteenth century is not known. Indirect evidence in the case of England suggests the decades 1460–80. It is clear, however, that during the sixteenth century population everywhere in Europe was growing.

Sometime in that period the population of Western Europe overtook the level achieved before the Black Death, although exactly when this occurred is obscured by the paucity of evidence surviving from both proto-statistical periods. Historians attempting to construct estimates of the total population of Europe generally agree that by 1600 population had regained the levels

TABLE 9.1   *The Population of Europe 1300–1600* (in millions)

	M. K. Bennett		Russell
1300	73		
1350	51	1348	54.4
1400	45	1400	35.4
1450	60	1450	–
1500	69	1500	–
1550	78	1550	45.7
1600	89	1600	–

Source: Slicher Van Bath, *The Agrarian History of Western Europe*, p. 80.

existing in 1300, although, as shown in Table 9.1, one source sees this as occurring prior to 1550 and another at about that date.

The general consensus is that the sixteenth century witnessed sustained demographic expansion throughout Western Europe. Despite the absence of hard statistical evidence, the conclusion of a noted historian is reassuring:

But while individual figures may be suspect, the overall picture which emerges from a synopsis of 16th century sources is perfectly clear in its outlines: all the evidence, statistical and other, points to a pronounced secular upswing in Europe's population.[1]

The absence of plague during the sixteenth century is perhaps a partial explanation for this phenomenon. Famines were not of major importance, at least when compared to those in the next century. Wars, on the other hand, were so prevalent that only twenty-five years of the sixteenth century were free of large-scale conflict somewhere in Europe. Nevertheless, population seemingly blossomed everywhere.

As the size of the total populace grew, so did the numbers of Europeans residing in cities. During the century the major cities of Western Europe outpaced any previous development. It is doubtful, however, that urbanization – or the percentage of the population living in cities – actually increased. Indeed, it more probably declined throughout the century. The expansion of large urban places was at the expense of the small market towns of the previous century.

While general population increase was typical of the entire sixteenth century, the seventeenth was subject to reverses. For Western Europe this was a grim epoch of wars, famine, and pestilence, each of which took its toll. Unlike the checks of the fourteenth century, however, the messengers of death during the seventeenth century visited the countries of Western Europe with differing severity and with differential results. Certain countries were terribly vulnerable to their visits, others were able to ward them off.

Germany, the Spanish Low Countries, Spain and perhaps Portugal lost population during the seventeenth century. The Thirty Years War (1618–48) devasted Germany. It was accompanied by dysentery, typhus, smallpox, plague and famine. Estimates of the fall in population (perhaps exaggerated when placed at almost 40 percent) seem to indicate that Germany's losses exceeded those of any other country.

Spain, and perhaps Portugal, suffered such population reverses, due to famine and plague, that Spain is estimated to have lost one-quarter of its population between 1600 and 1700. The Spanish Netherlands provided a favorite battleground for warring European nations during the century, so that Brabant, for example, had only a few more inhabitants at the end of the century than it had in 1526. The rest of the Spanish Netherlands probably fared as badly. It is interesting that most of the population decline occurred in the countryside; urban places were so little affected that Ghent actually grew in numbers, as did Liege. Reversing its spectacular decline in the 1570s and 1580s, Antwerp resumed a steady growth.

Apart from those countries suffering clear losses, a number of others at

---

[1] Karl F. Helleiner, 'The Population of Europe from the Black Death to the Eve of the Vital Revolution', *Cambridge Economic History*, vol. 4, pp. 22–3.

best stagnated during the period, Italy and France being the most notable of these. Again the Malthusian checks of famine and plague were responsible. Like the Spanish Netherlands, Italy was a continual battleground; famines there became commonplace, and the plagues of 1630–1 and 1656–7 were so devastating that the population of Italy in 1700 was no greater than it had been in 1600.

The seventeenth-century French population also endured famines, plagues, or both during 1628–38, 1646–52, 1674–5 and 1679, and in 1693–4 a famine so severe as to be termed 'great'. The nation additionally lost 175,000 Protestants who fled for religious reasons. After the first quarter of the century, which may have brought some increase, the trend in French population appears to have been downhill until at the end of the century it was probably no higher than during the first quarter.

While France and Italy were stagnating, the Dutch Republic and England were actually experiencing an expansion of population. The United Provinces of the Netherlands, unlike the Spanish-dominated Low Countries, were notably successful in repelling human invaders, although their defenses fell before the onslaught of plague, which struck there in 1623–5, 1635–7, 1654–5 and 1663–4. Also the bitter struggle against the French, particularly in 1672, resulted in some territorial devastation. Nevertheless, recovery was quick and it is generally believed that the population of the United Provinces grew substantially during the century. Part of this growth was due to a positive natural rate of increase, but part also was due to a hospitable attitude toward immigration, as the Dutch opened up their doors to foreigners – not only to fellow Protestants, but also to Iberian Jews. Urbanization grew even faster, until in Holland (the most urbanized of the provinces) 60 percent of the population were townspeople as early as 1622. Dutch cities throve and expanded throughout most of the century.

The other important country which gained population during the seventeenth century was England, despite the onslaught of plagues, such as those that struck London in 1603, 1625, 1636–7 and in 1665. Their total impact proved less severe than the two Italian epidemics, and the population of England and Wales had doubtless grown larger by 1700 than it was in 1600. For illustrative purposes, one popular estimate for the English population during the seventeenth century shows an increase of 25 percent during the century. The population of 1600 is estimated to have been 4.8 million; in 1630, 5.6 million; in 1670, 5.8 million; and in 1700, 6.1 million, although these figures are probably too high.

In summary then, it appears that population everywhere in Europe grew during the sixteenth century, but that the picture changed sharply during the second century of the modern era. The Dutch United Provinces and England and Wales continued to gain population during the seventeenth century, but the populations of Italy and France stagnated during that century and those of the Spanish Netherlands, Spain, perhaps Portugal and Germany actually declined.

II

The history of prices parallels the history of population. The sixteenth century witnessed dramatic increases in the level and changes in the pattern of prices everywhere in Western Europe. So significant was the increase in the absolute level of prices and in the lag of wages behind other prices that this era is known as the 'price revolution'. Inflation swept throughout Western Europe with the general price level climbing 200 to 300 percent higher in 1600 than it had been in 1500. Prices in Spain, for example, at the end of the century were 3.4 times higher than at the beginning; in France 2.2 times; England 2.6; in Leyden, the Dutch textile city, 3.0; and in Alsace, Italy and Sweden prices had approximately doubled. Such a

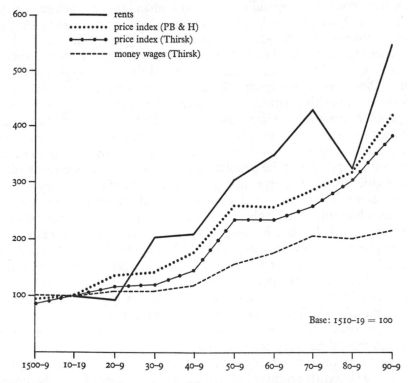

Fig. 9.1.   The aggregate price index and indices of rents and wages in England: 1500–1600.
Sources: Thirsk, *The Agrarian History of England and Wales*, vol. 4, pp. 862, 865; Phelps-Brown and Hopkins, 'Wage-rates and Prices: Evidence for Population Pressure in the Sixteenth Century', p. 306; Kerridge, 'The Movement of Rent, 1540–1640', p. 25.

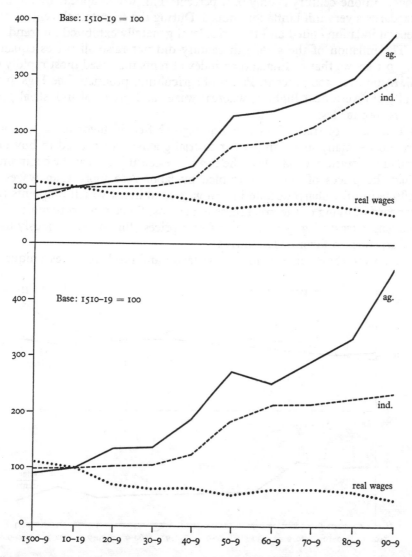

Fig. 9.2a.   Price indices of agricultural and industrial goods and real wages in England: 1500–1600.
   Source: Thirsk, *The Agrarian History of England and Wales*, vol. 4, pp. 862, 865.
Fig. 9.2b.   Price indices of agricultural and industrial goods and real wages in England: 1500–1600.
   Sources: Phelps-Brown and Hopkins, 'Wage-Rates and Prices: Evidence for Population Pressure in the Sixteenth Century'. p. 306; and 'Seven Centuries of the Prices of Consumables, Compared with Builders' Wage-Rates', pp. 311–14.

general increase in the level of prices appears more dramatic than in fact it was, since the annual rate of increase which will allow the price level to double in one century is only 0.72 percent. This would appear by modern standards a very mild inflation indeed. During the seventeenth century the general inflation ended and the price level generally exhibited no trend.

The inflation of the sixteenth century did not raise all prices equally. Fig. 9.1 shows that in England an index of rents increased most rapidly of all, rising over 500 percent. Prices of agricultural products (see Figs. 9.2a and 9.2b) were next highest, whereas wages and prices of industrial products rose far less.

The terms of trade shown in Fig. 9.3a shifted in favor of agricultural products – many more units of industrial goods were needed to buy one unit of agricultural products at the end of the century than at the beginning. That the prices of goods consumed by labor rose more than wages is reflected in the sharp decline in real wages, an index which pinpoints the standard of living of the great mass of persons. Since rents rose most of all and wages least (Fig. 9.1), relative factor prices (Fig. 9.3b) obviously took a sharp turn in favor of landowners.

Nor were these changes in relative factor and product prices unique to

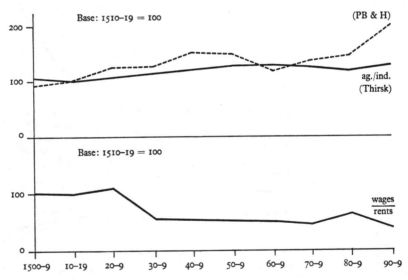

Fig. 9.3a. The terms of trade between agriculture and industrial prices in England: 1500–1600.
Sources: Thirsk, *The Agrarian History of England and Wales*, vol. 4, pp. 862, 865; Phelps-Brown and Hopkins, 'Wage-rates and Prices: Evidence for Population Pressure in the Sixteenth Century', p. 306.
Fig. 9.7b. The ratio between wages and rents in England: 1500–1600.
Sources: Thirsk, *The Agrarian History of England and Wales*, vol. 4, pp. 862, 865; Kerridge, 'The Movement of Rent, 1540–1640', p. 25.

England, for which the best quantitative information is available. The evidence reproduced in Figs. 9.4 and 9.5 shows that the changes occurring in England were general throughout Western Europe. In Germany, France and Spain the terms of trade also shifted in favor of agriculture, while real wages declined significantly, and the changes in relative factor prices seem everywhere to have been similar. Rents in France appear to have risen 380 percent during the course of the century, while the wages of labor increased only 130 percent.

In sum, the general rise in price level during the sixteenth century was universal. Relative product and factor prices also changed in similar patterns. The prices of agricultural goods increased relative to manufactured goods and rents of land increased more rapidly than wages. The real wages of labor declined significantly.

III

The similar patterns we have just pointed out were matched by other phenomena common to all of Western Europe during the sixteenth century. For one thing, the volume of trade expanded everywhere, especially in the flourishing international commerce of Northern Europe. European vessels in increasing numbers moved along the traditional water routes, voyaging to the Mediterranean and most dramatically venturing into the great oceans to traffic with the alien continents of Asia and the New World. At the beginning of the century, the center of this commerce was still concentrated in Northern Italy, where the city-states of Milan, Florence, Genoa and Venice and their lesser neighbors specialized in manufacturing and trade. From these cities the rest of Europe initially drew their supplies of Mediterranean goods and valuable commodities from the East. In this area a lively and expanding traffic was maintained in grain, salt and salted foods (mainly fish), as well as in oil, wine and cheese. Other ships were laden with wool, raw silk and leather destined for manufactured goods. The trade in minerals was of minor, but growing, importance as a demand appeared for alum, coral, iron and copper. The Mediterranean thus bore rich and varied cargoes throughout the sixteenth century.

Historically, however, the most vital Mediterranean trade was not of local origin, but came through a long chain of overland commercial exchanges from India, Ceylon and Indonesia. In the fabled spice trade, pepper outranked even nutmeg and cloves in importance. Bales of Chinese and Persian silks, Indian cottons, Chinese rhubarb and precious stones supplemented the exotic traffic which aroused the envy of all Europe and made Venice, where the trade centered, one of the world's great seaports.

The geographical monopoly over this luxury trade, held during the Middle Ages by Mediterranean merchants, was challenged early in the

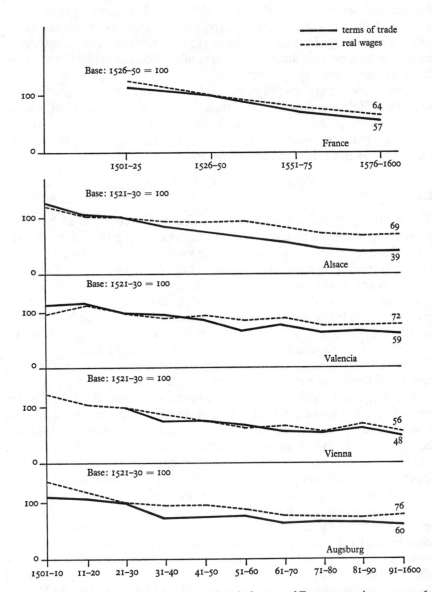

Fig. 9.4. Indices of real wages and terms of trade for several European regions: 1500–1600.
Sources: Phelps-Brown and Hopkins, 'Wage-Rates and Prices: Evidence for Population Pressure in the Sixteenth Centuryl, pp. 305–6; and 'Builders' Wage-Rates, Prices and Population: Some Further Evidence', *Economica*, 26, no. 101, pp. 35–8.

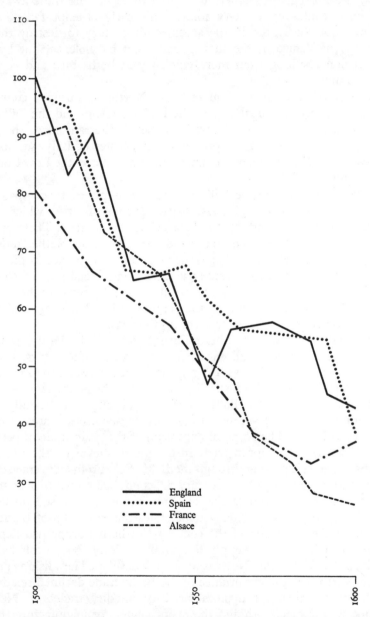

Fig. 9.5. Indices of real wages during the sixteenth century for England, Spain, France and Alsace.

Source: Phelps-Brown and Hopkins, 'Builders' Wage-Rates and Population: Some Further Evidence', pp. 18–38.

sixteenth century by Portugal. Pushing through the Atlantic waters to India, the Portuguese seamen attempted to divert the trade away from traditional routes by military force. This early attempt failed, and it remained for the Dutch in the seventeenth century to destroy the pre-eminence of Venice in the luxury trade, not by violence, but by price competition resulting from more efficiency in both ships and economic organization.

The sixteenth-century commerce of Northern Europe, connecting England, France, Portugal, Spain, the Low Countries and the Baltic, was initially a smaller cousin to the trade of the Mediterranean. As the Mediterranean region boosted the productive city-states of Italy, so Northern Europe depended on a manufacturing-trading center in the Low Countries of Holland and Flanders.

While Northern Europe still had no urban places to compare with Venice or Genoa, it did give rise to two groups of cities, which, at the beginning of the sixteenth century, specialized in sea trade. These were the towns of the North German Hanse and the ports of the Netherlands. The Netherlands' city of Antwerp, gradually gaining dominance as the harbor of Bruges silted up, had become the chief commercial port of Northern Europe during the sixteenth century, until it was destroyed in the changing fortunes of war. By the end of the century it had been replaced in importance by Amsterdam, a few miles up the coast.

The major trades of Northern Europe were in the hardy, cold-zone products of grain, salt and salted fish, in woolen cloth, furs, iron and timber. The grain trade was a regular exchange between the importers – Spain, Portugal and the industrialized regions of the Netherlands – and the exporters, France and the Baltic. The trade developed sufficiently during the century to permit supplies to go also to some other areas suffering temporary dearth. The scope of expansion of the grain trade in particular and of Northern European trade in general is shown by the rise in the number of vessels passing through the Baltic Sea. From an average of 1300 a year at the beginning of the century the count had grown to over 5000 by the end. Since the average size of ships had also increased during this period, the comparison actually understates the expansion of Baltic commerce. At the beginning of the century Northern Europe had depended wholly on the Baltic to supply one vital article of food – salt fish and, particularly, salt herring. Now, as the Dutch developed new fishing grounds in the North Sea, the importance of the Baltic trade declined relatively.

The most important manufactured commodity traded in Northern Europe was woolen cloth and the major centers of manufacture (besides Northern Italy) were in Northern France, Flanders, Brabant, Holland and Eastern England. Flanders was far and away the most outstanding of these, with its trade centered at Antwerp for the first three-quarters of the century. Raw wool to be woven in Flanders was imported mostly from Spain and England, but England also exported woven cloth on a large scale to Antwerp and to the Baltic. These, however, were chiefly undyed and unfinished fabrics which had to be further processed by the importers.

Meanwhile, an independent trade was thriving along the Atlantic Coast, where Spain, England, France and the Netherlands were engaging in brisk exchanges of wool, cloth, wine and salt. During the century this trade tended to join together the greater commercial loops of the Mediterranean and the Baltic regions until the three links became one chain of commerce.

The establishment of a regular trade between Europe and the rest of the inhabited world was a major achievement of the sixteenth century. Once viewed primarily as a source of fish, by the end of the sixteenth century the ocean had become a king's highway, where voyages between Lisbon and India, or Seville and the West Indies were almost commonplace. Clearly, the most important of the oceanic trades was between Spain and the New World, following the mid-century discovery of the world's richest silver mines, whose wealth could endow not only Spain, but all of Europe.

IV

We have reached a point now where our earlier sketches of the sixteenth century's population, prices and commerce can be brought together to show the dominant patterns of economic development for that century, The fact that in Western Europe the trend in absolute and relative prices and in population growth was everywhere the same makes our task relatively simple and emphasizes that growth in population, both geographically and temporally, was the key. Population grew and, early in the century diminishing returns to additional laborers were encountered. As population continued to expand, the wages of labor fell relative to the price of land. Agricultural goods rose in price relative to industrial goods, because agriculture used relatively large amounts of the increasingly expensive factor, land.

In the monetary field, the rise in all prices, both of products and of factors, was due partly to the increased quantity of money coined from newly developed European mines and the importation of silver from the New World and partly to the quickened commercial pace. The Spanish monopoly of this import also led to an increased volume of international trade, since the rise in bullion imports to Spain increased prices there and made it an attractive place to sell goods and services and a relatively unattractive place to purchase goods. Armies, weapons and luxury goods were purchased by the Spanish, who settled accounts by exporting to the other countries of Europe their hoards of silver from the New World.

How much this stimulated international trade is difficult to assess, for

New World treasure was accompanied by another (perhaps more important) factor – the general growth in sixteenth-century population, which reduced the costs of using the market to allocate resources. As a consequence of this availability of the market, new secondary institutional arrangements sprang up, which allowed specialization in production and exchange while reinforcing the different comparative advantages of different regions. In such fertile soil, foreign trade flourished and blossomed in every branch, nourished particularly by such fast-growing urban markets as Antwerp and London. Meanwhile, smaller local and regional markets, unable to compete with their more efficient rivals, were in a state of decline.

The rise of a few major markets is explained by the nature of the market itself. In the process of producing transactions, a market generates information about the prices at which exchanges can be made. Since these prices are available to all who are present, anyone can decide whether to buy or sell, and this one source of productivity gain is probably paramount among all the obvious advantages of a single market. During periods of expanding trade the larger markets are the more efficient because of economies of scale involved in transactions. Thus centrally located urban places gained at the expense of their less fortunately situated rivals in the intra-market competition for traders.

The introduction into our analysis of a transaction sector linking the agricultural and industrial sectors with each other and with the final consumer complicates any statement we can make about consumer welfare during the sixteenth century. It is clear that the direct influence of population growth under conditions of diminishing returns was to reduce the overall efficiency of the economy, leading to a decline in *per capita* income everywhere. Indirectly, however, population growth would have also exerted the opposite effect, of raising productivity and increasing *per capita* income, because in widening the market it stimulated trade and commerce.

The increased efficiency of the transaction sector influenced relative product prices and the terms of trade in exactly the same way as did a growing population. The consumer prices of agricultural goods would fall less, relative to the prices of the factors of production, than would those of industrial products, which were perfectly elastic in supply. Thus the terms of trade recorded in the market would shift in favor of farm products. The relative increase in farm prices was due both to a decline in agricultural productivity, which lowered incomes, and to an increase in efficiency in exchanging farm products, which tended to raise incomes. The welfare of the society would depend upon which effect dominated in any given time or situation.

In sum, the balance sheet for the sixteenth century shows a decline in productivity in agriculture, constant productivity in manufacture and increasing productivity in the transaction sector of the market. The material well-being of Western Europe depended on whether the increasing efficiency of the market could offset the productivity declines in agriculture due to diminishing returns. Generally, the outcome was not happy, diminishing returns dominated and Western Europe moved into the seventeenth century suffering from Malthusian checks. Famines and plagues once more swept the nations of Europe.

V

As we have seen in our earlier discussion of population, the seventeenth-century impact of these disasters was selective, unlike the devastation in the fourteenth century. Some areas, such as England, emerged relatively unscathed, while others, like Spain, were decimated. It is fair to assume that the efficiency of economic organization played a large part in determining the effectiveness of the Malthusian checks. This is the significant difference between the fourteenth century, when the economies of Western Europe were all organized quite uniformly, and the seventeenth century, by which time institutions and property rights within the emerging nation-states had been taking divergent paths for 100 or 200 years.

During the sixteenth century the commerce of Western Europe evolved not within a peaceful, orderly, free-trade world, but against all the obstacles that could be reared by war, hostility, and jealousy between the rival nation-states. The heads of state were certain that they could extend their influence only at the expense of some other sovereign, and they were equally persuaded that an economy could extend its commerce only at the expense of another nation. One prime example of this philosophy was the abortive attempt of the Portuguese to divert the spice trade by force of arms. Other political units attempted by more or less overt means to regulate both internal and external economic relations. From the urgent need to provide the revenues required to engage in the great national struggles of the early modern era was born the age of mercantilism.

The key to mercantilism comprised the factors described in the previous chapter. The results were highly diverse policies, which led to sharply different consequences in the seventeenth century. The economic events of this century therefore must (to some extent at least) be examined according to national boundaries. No longer will a single population model explain the major economic developments occurring in Europe.

By the beginning of the seventeenth century population change had become but one of the important parameters influencing economic growth. The emergence and nature of any given nation-state and the extent and efficiency of its market all assumed vital roles as co-determining factors. The nations of Western Europe were ambivalent in their relations one with another, drawn together by the hope of gains from mutual trading, yet divided by the desire of each state to dominate.

Against such a background of tension let us briefly consider how prices fared during the seventeenth century in the Netherlands, England, France and Spain – the four rival giants among European nations. We shall be particularly interested in the course of real wages and in determining which factors dominated changes in their levels. While the evidence we present here is immensely better than that extant for earlier centuries, our conclusions must still be considered tentative.

The seven northern provinces of the Low Countries were united into the Dutch Republic after the successful conclusion of an agonizing eighty years (1568–1648) of revolt against Spain. Even during that time the Dutch had prospered. Real wages (Fig. 9.6a), declining in the sixteenth century as

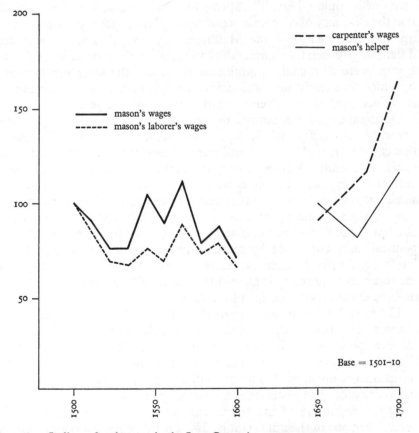

Fig. 9.6a. Indices of real wages in the Low Countries: 1500–1700.
Sources: H. Van der Wee, *The Growth of the Antwerp Market and the European Economy* (Martinus Nijhoff, 1963), vol. 1, p. 543; N. W. Posthumus, *Lakenhandel*, vol. 2, pp. 217, 1014–17.

116

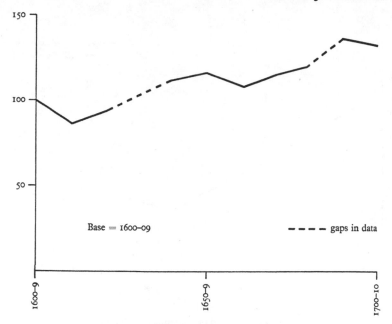

Fig. 9.6*b*.   An index of real wages in England: 1600–1700.
Source: Phelps-Brown and Hopkins, 'Seven Centuries of the Prices of Consumables, Compared with Builders' Wage-Rates', 296–314.

everywhere, revived during the seventeenth century and increased approximately 50 percent during its last three quarters. It is possible that better wage data (especially for the period 1600 to 1625) might show the rise in real wages as even more spectacular. Moreover, the improvement occurred despite a steady increase in population. In England too, recovery from the nadir of the sixteenth century began during the seventeenth. Real wages in England (Fig. 9.6*b*) increased by 36.5 percent between the two periods 1601–10 and 1711–20. Real income *per capita* doubtless increased during the century at the same time that population grew.

For perhaps the first time in the history of Western Europe, both the Dutch and the British economies had succeeded in increasing the *per capita* income of a growing population despite the continued pressure of diminishing returns in agriculture. Clearly, productivity was growing more rapidly in some or all sectors than was population. This phenomenon will be examined in Chapters 10 and 11.

It is apparent that the French were not as successful as either the Dutch or the English. An index of real wages in France fell from an average level of 44 (Fig. 9.6*c*) during 1551–75 to 34 during 1576–1600; it then revived to 42 during the first quarter of the seventeenth century and fluctuated around an average of 41 for the entire century. France was not able significantly to

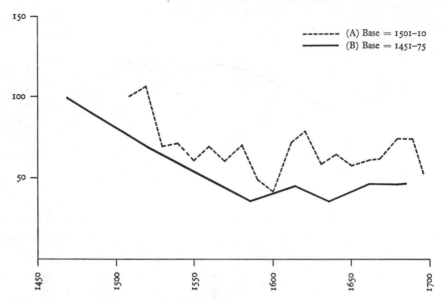

Fig. 9.6c.   An index of real wages in France during the seventeenth century.
Sources: (A) Builders' wages divided by the price of wheat, M. Baulant, 'Le Salaire des Ouvriers du Batiment à Paris de 1400 à 1726', *Annules*, 26 annee no. 2, pp. 463–81; and 'Le Prix des Grains à Paris de 1481 à 1788', *Annales*, 25 annee no. 3, pp. 520–40; (B) Phelps-Brown and Hopkins. 'Wage-Rates and Prices: Evidence for Population Pressure in the Sixteenth Century', pp. 281–306.

improve the well-being of her inhabitants during the century, even though the level of population was static or perhaps declining.

Even worse was the lot of Spain, a clear loser in terms of the well-being of her people. Population changes continued to dominate the economy: when the plagues struck and population declined, real wages rose (Fig. 9*d*); when population increased again, real wages fell. The plagues that struck in 1589–91, 1629–31, 1650–4 and 1694 brought improvement in real wages; but only at such a tragic cost could the retarded Spanish economy effect that betterment. It lacked strength to counter the effects of population growth.

The evidence for the seventeenth century thus suggests a differential pattern of economic growth between the countries of Western Europe. The United Provinces and England succeed for the first time in achieving a rising standard of living in the face of a growing population. The rest of the nations follow the now familiar pattern of economic welfare and population growth moving in opposite directions. We shall, in subsequent chapters, examine the peculiar characteristics exhibited by the winners and losers in the race to achieve long-run sustained growth.

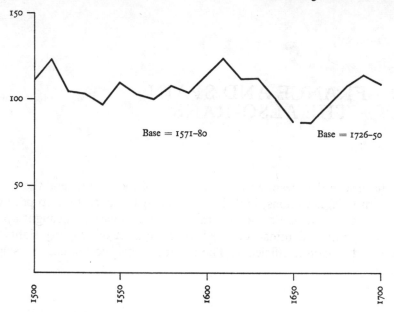

Fig. 9.6d. An index of real wages in Spain.

Sources: Earl J. Hamilton, *American Treasure and the Price Revolution in Spain, 1501–1650* (Octagon Books, 1965), p. 279; and *War and Prices in Spain, 1651–1800* (Harvard University Press, 1947), p. 215.

These two series, 1500–1650 and 1650–1700, cannot strictly be compared because of two different bases. However, we believe that they are accurately joined above.

10. FRANCE AND SPAIN – THE ALSO-RANS

We have seen that despite the magnificence of their courts and the scale of their imperial ambitions, both France and Spain failed to keep pace with the Netherlands and England. Both absolutist monarchies, caught up in a race for political dominance, failed to create a set of property rights that promoted economic efficiency. The result for their economies was stagnation.

I

We must return to earlier centuries to pick up the story of French political history. The dismal period of the Hundred Years War saw not only invading English armies occupying parts of France and marauding bands of mercenaries preying on the countryside, but also seemingly endless squabbles among the great nobles themselves. France was a country in name only when Charles VI died in 1422 after agreeing to accept the king of England as his heir. A rival, the Dauphin Charles, had backers for his claim to the throne among the Armagnac nobles outside the English- and Burgundian-controlled territory of what today we consider France. He faced the awesome task of recovering more than half his claimed kingdom from the hands of the English and Burgundians – a task which required desperate and expensive expedients. During Charles' first years as king, he found it necessary to call repeatedly on the national Estates General for their co-operation in obtaining the necessary fiscal measures. While the *Gabelle* had been collected without consent since 1383, additional sources of revenue, such as the *Taille*, *Aides*, and forced loans, were periodically requested by the king, but always with the awareness that too heavy a tax burden would push his subjects into the camp of his enemies. The king's troubles did not stop there, because ultimately it was the regional and local assemblies that actually provided the funds, so Charles VII was forced to go directly there after obtaining a 'grant' from the national assemblies.

The rival rulers of France were in direct competition for the support of the citizenry. Both the duke of Bedford, controlling the English-held part of France, and John the Fearless, duke of Burgundy, were, like Charles, circumscribed by the actions of rivals in their taxing power. In 1418, when John the Fearless failed to collect the *Aides* in that part of France which he controlled, Charles, the Valois king, was forced to be similarly generous in his part of France in order to retain the loyalty of his 'subjects'.

The turning point in this contest for power appears to have occurred in 1428 when the English assaulted Orleans. This threat permitted Charles to raise 500,000 livre tournois from the assembly he had called at Chenon. This fiscal support plus the dramatic appearance and success of Joan of Arc in raising the siege of Orleans and then inducing the dauphin to be crowned at Reims turned the tide in favor of the French king. Neither the English nor the Burgundians were ever to be as powerful in France. Charles' hand was strengthened in receiving regular tax monies but challenges to his authority remained. Even after making peace with the Burgundians in 1435 and while his fortunes steadily improved in his struggles with the English, problems developed with marauding bands of unemployed soldiers and mercenaries. Charles, while successful in eliminating close competitors for his throne, was at the same time still in a position to raise substantial sums from his subjects in order to rid the countryside of the scourging effects of military brigands. No rival state or noble survived who was able to perform this task. Thus Charles obtained a monopoly of protection in France. Increasingly in the 1430s the king treated *Aides*, like the *Gabelle*, as his prerogative, a tax to be levied without consent. The assembly at Orleans in 1439, proved to be the last national assembly to approve the *Taille*. While Charles VII did appeal for funds from local assemblies as late as 1451, the king's control over taxing power had actually become complete after 1439. The Estates General had surrendered control over taxing power in the process of providing Charles VII with the finances to maintain an army that would defend the borders and eliminate the marauders from within.

In this process of reclaiming France, Charles instituted a set of military reforms which, by establishing a permanent organization of twenty regular companies of heavy cavalry, created a professional army, the main advantage of which was that it did away with the need to rely entirely upon un-trustworthy mercenaries. Charles supported these troops with the purchase of cannons and the importation of trained artillery men on an unprecedented scale. The results were a reversal of the defeats the French had suffered from the English in earlier times and, ultimately, a successful conclusion to the Hundred Years War. By 1453, the English had been driven almost entirely from French soil.

Despite the emerging dominance of the French Crown, regional areas of France continued to be somewhat isolated from each other. Local and provincial Estates General did continue to meet and have local taxing power. It was not until the Wars of Religion in the next century that there was an abortive attempt to revive the former role of the Estates General.

The meeting of the Estates General at Blois in 1576–7 was perhaps the last chance to peaceably reverse the trend toward absolute royal control.

The end of the sixteenth century saw the religious wars and the return of anarchy to the provinces involved. The Huguenots were a substantial threat to the king, at times seizing control of a province and appropriating the royal revenues. Nevertheless, the Crown eventually triumphed, the warfare serving once again to demonstrate to the French the value of peace. When the wars were over, the Crown, as the keeper of the peace, also held undisputed sway over the tax structure.

We have dwelt at length on the era of Charles VII because it is clear that the absolute royal control over fiscal power developed during this period. The result of the virtual elimination of close rivals to the state from within and the intensification of competition with rivals from without was a dramatic increase in taxes under Louis XI (approximately a fourfold increase during his reign); perhaps some decline under Louis XII; and a rise again in the early sixteenth century under Francis I. Over the whole of the Renaissance, the *Taille* increased from 1.2 million to 11 million livre tournois in current prices (or approximately two to threefold in real terms).

Accompanying the growth of the royal power to tax was another aspect of Crown fiscal policy which was to have a crucial impact on the structure of property rights. This was the sale of public offices in the expanding bureaucracy. The immediate consequence of the sale of offices was to increase Crown revenue and, by the time of Francis I, it had become a major aspect of the French fiscal system. Not only were the major and minor official positions (including the judiciary) for sale, but many useless offices with no duties were also sold. They did more than confer a title upon the receiver. Typically, the holder was also exempt from the *Taille*, *Aides* and the *Gabelle*. Thus an office, to the holder, was of considerable value aside from the income it offered.

The fiscal system of Renaissance France was carried over, elaborated, and codified (or perhaps ossified) under the *Ancien Régime* during the seventeenth century. Richelieu and Colbert did not change the basic fiscal structure. They treated it as a foundation and built upon it a more elaborate edifice, which structured property rights in France in great detail. The key to understanding the structure of property rights in the *Ancien Régime* is to comprehend that royal control over taxation was absolute and a vast bureaucracy was dependent on royal favor.

II

The fiscal policy of the French Crown, whether intentionally or not, did almost everything conceivable to thwart the spread of an extensive market and thereby surrendered the gains that lay therein. Regions were artificially separated, isolated one from another by a system of internal tariffs. Market areas generally did not extend beyond the vicinity of a few big cities and certain outports. Probably France during the *Ancien Régime* should be considered as composed of more than thirty separate market areas. Of these, only Paris drew upon a substantial hinterland; the rest of France drew their supplies from neighboring areas.

However, France was not without its urban places. Paris after all was one of the commanding cities of Europe. Rouen, which can be considered the outport of Paris, was perhaps the second city of the kingdom. Other important cities were Lyons, Marseilles, and lesser places such as Tours, Blois and Orleans. Lyons in particular deserves mention since it was one of the great international centers of monetary and commercial transactions. In particular, Lyons served as the center of French foreign financial dealings.

While France engaged in foreign trade, exporting wine, corn and cloth, this was of minor importance to the economy. Perhaps as much as 90 percent of the wine produced was consumed in France itself. Partly as a result of domestic policies and partly due to its large size and the diversity of its resources, France came close to enjoying complete autarchy.

Even within these restricted regional markets, access to the market was restricted. Monopolies, guilds, and even the right to sell certain types of agricultural outputs, were considered privileges. Such rights were valuable to the holders, hence a fruitful source of government revenue. It appears to have been state policy to keep the markets of France within a reasonable administrative size.

III

The trend toward the breaking up of the demesne began in the twelfth century and by the beginning of the early modern period the nobility was largely removed from direct control over the land. The French nobility lived mostly on the dues collected from their peasants in the form of fixed rents and prerogatives. France throughout this period remained a nation of peasants, with rural property divided between a very large number of peasants and numerous petty nobility, who cultivated part of their lands and received fixed rents from the rest. The monarchy during this era supported the hereditary tenures of the peasants, in essence giving the tenants legal ownership subject only to the fixed rent payment.

The techniques employed in agriculture remained basically medieval – a two- or three-course rotation in lands divided into a multitude of separate plots. Wheat and rye were the staple crops and, where the climate made it possible, vineyards were cultivated. Wine was produced in almost every region of France. Most of it must have been of very low quality. The fact that it was locally grown and not imported from the best producing areas is ample testimony to the restricted domestic market in France.

During the sixteenth century the growth in population led to severe diminishing returns and raised the value of land as it reduced the value of labor. The inflation of the sixteenth century significantly reduced the value of the fixed rents received by the nobility, to the benefit of the tenants. The nobility in turn sought with some success to revive and rejuvenate the traditional rights and obligations of the *seigneurie*. The peasants, who should have been the main beneficiaries of the inflation, in turn near the end of the century suffered the ravages of the Wars of Religion. The benefits of expropriation via the price system were also tempered by the decline in real wages. The members of the working class, who lived on their wages, were reduced to severe poverty.

The peasant was also subjected to the *Tailles*, *Gabelle* and *Aides*. These were not fixed by custom, but as we have seen were increased at the will of the Crown. This method of taxation required a significant bureaucracy to collect it. In the end, the peasant paid for this widespread civil service. The monarchy, using its bureaucracy, took the place of the *seigneurie* in administrating local justice.

No major enclosure movement occurred in France, with the exception of Normandy. The incentives provided by a limited market and the costs of changing a legal system clogged with bureaucrats outweighed the benefits to any individual landowner or voluntary group. The benefits to the society were of course much greater, but the mechanism did not exist to bring this source of gain to fruition. Some enclosure, however, did occur, the surviving commons and wastes being enclosed, but the small strips successfully resisted all attempts. During the early modern period France made little progress toward a more efficient reorganization of its arable land.

During the sixteenth century sharecropping (*metayage*) was increasingly used as the means of organizing agriculture. Sharecropping had been employed much earlier in vineyards, but after 1500 it spread to other agricultural areas in France until it existed everywhere. The landlord received a portion of the crop as his rent and the tenant kept the rest. The landlords' portion generally varied from one-quarter to one-half of the output. While present everywhere, *metayage* is particularly associated in the literature with the poorer regions of France. Often the poverty of the region is attributed to sharecropping. Recently this has been theoretically shown not to be the case; share cropping is neither more nor less efficient than other types of agricultural contracts, such as, say, fixed rent contracts.

Sharecropping was considered less efficient because the output was shared. The landlord provided the land, the tenant the labor; the land was fixed in amount, but the tenant could provide as much labor as he wished. The more he supplied, the higher the output, but a portion of the output belonged to the lord. Thus, as with a tax, the peasant received less for his labor than the value which he produced, which is the same thing as relatively raising the value of his leisure; hence, the tenant would devote too few units of labor and the maximum economic value of the land would not be achieved. The tenants' incentive to work or invest in the land was reduced by the nature of the rent payment. The same disincentive was supposed to influence the amount of capital invested in the land.

This view ignores the fact that in the lease the landlord could specify the amount of labor and capital that must be applied to the land. Should the tenant fail to live up to the contract, he faced eviction. One of the important developments prior to the widespread use of *metayage* was the securing of property rights in land. The widespread introduction of this system required secure property rights. The owner had to be known and his right to the land acknowledged. This situation had developed in France at the same time as the establishment of the nation state.

Since the share and the amount of capital and labor employed on the land were subject to negotiation, and the contract could be enforced, *metayage* was as efficient as any other system. It did not matter whether, for example, the landlord required the peasant to invest more in the land and then charged a lower percentage of the crop, or whether he invested in the land himself and charged a higher percentage. The investment, if profitable, would be made. Nor could the landlord charge a percentage so high that the tenant could make more elsewhere or he would lose his peasants to that alternative. Whether under *metayage* or under a fixed rent contract, the peasant obtained the market value of his labor and the landlord the value of the rent, neither more nor less. *Metayage* was not responsible for the poverty existing in France. We must look elsewhere for an explanation.

The policy of taxation that developed also had an important influence upon the distribution of land holdings throughout early modern France. The nobility and office holders paid no taxes on their land or property. Thus land was worth more to these persons than to anyone not so privileged. A basis for trade, sale and conversion was created and large land holdings were assembled. The rehabilitation of the large estate which has often been noted (although the extent of the process was exaggerated by French historians) can be explained in this manner. It is a mistake to suggest that France in the early modern period was a country of large estates. It was not. The small peasant proprietor was typical.

The poverty of French agriculture which developed during the early modern period was the result of diminishing returns and an institutional environment that frustrated efficient adjustments and the innovation of new techniques. The restrictions which kept a national market from developing were primarily responsible for the fact that French agriculture during the early modern period remained heavily medieval in character.

The history of industrial regulation in France is an oft-told story. The development of a vast bureaucracy loyal to the Crown was one part of the regulatory system and the other was the strengthening of the guilds and their use as the principal agent of government regulation. The Edicts of 1581 (Henry III), 1597 (Henry IV) and 1673 (Louis XIV – actually inspired by Colbert) were to provide the principal guidelines. Enforcement of the first two edicts was less effective than of the last, which enabled Colbert to bring the guild system into its own. 'Briefly the programme consisted in making the guild the universal model for the structure of trade not only in the cities but also in the market towns and even in the country.'[1] Thus a twofold administrative machinery, the guilds and industrial officials, became the backbone of the detailed regulation of almost every aspect of manufacturing and commercial life. The former were supported by the courts, even when their medieval and restrictive regulation occasionally ran counter to the government inspectors. The guilds were the foundation of the industrial organization of France.

State regulation evolved to the point where it often covered every detail of the production process of an industry. In the case of the dyeing of cloth, for example, the regulations ran to 317 articles. Regulations were created after consultation with guild officials and generally mirrored medieval production techniques. The system of control and inspection by guild officials could be so comprehensive that, during the time of Colbert, even ordinary cloth required at least six inspections.

The basic objective of the state was fiscal. In effect, the state perpetuated and enforced guild monopolies in return for revenues. The guilds purchased their monopoly rights from the Crown. This was a valuable Crown prerogative. When in 1597 the king was in particular financial distress and in arrears in paying his Swiss troops, the chief of the Swiss guards, as a remedy, was actually appointed to sell guild masters' rights. The price of a monopoly or other privileges could be changed, especially in a national emergency. Colbert's edict of 1673, for example, explicitly linked the enormous current expenses with a new scale of charges. In 1691 a royal charge was specifically laid on guild masters.

The French did more in the direction of establishing property rights in knowledge. The Crown granted exclusive rights to investors for various periods of time and no doubt some of these were productive, but the king's advisors were generally looking for artistic and luxury goods, rather than those that might increase the efficiency of more mundane industries. No new invention in any event could conflict with existing grants. If a new invention would damage an existing monopoly, the Crown could not grant a monopoly without violating prior grants. A grant when obtained was

[1] Eli Hecksher, *Mercantilism*, rev. ed. edited by E. F. Soderlund, (Allen and Unwin, 1955), vol. I, p. 145.

often only for a limited market area, rather than the whole of France. The process of invention was not substantially encouraged in France during this time by these actions.

The consequences for economic efficiency in the French industrial system were that (1) mobility of labor was everywhere circumscribed, and entry into an industry was difficult if not impossible; (2) mobility of capital was equally circumscribed; (3) innovation was everywhere stifled or prohibited by the minute regulation of the production process that did not permit deviation from custom; and (4) in many cases, such as the Edict of 1571, prices of every type of cloth were fixed.

If the system of guild control together with royal inspection was not enough to stifle economic growth, royal sponsored and subsidized industry added to the ossification of the French economy. While France became famous for its crown-sponsored artistic and luxury industries, few managed to survive in the absence of royal subsidy. In short, royal favor often supported inefficient industries. What was true of royal industries was equally applicable to foreign trading companies.

IV

The failure of the French economy to exhibit long-run sustained economic growth was a failure of the French state to develop an efficient set of property rights. The factor markets, except for the capital market, moved ahead. Property rights in land were established and protected. Land became transferable and labor remained free of its servile obligations. The product market, on the other hand, continued as the result of state policy to be as imperfect as during the late Middle Ages. Guilds and monopolies and the protection of local markets continued. As a result, the gains available from the transaction sector were lost to the French economy.

V

The similarities between French and Spanish political developments are striking. In both cases we observe that the representative bodies gave up effective control over taxation in return for stability and order; in both the Crown gradually obtained a degree of monopoly power which enabled it alone to alter the tax structure and set the amounts payable. There are other similarities. In both countries political unification took a long time to complete, some areas stubbornly retained a degree of local autonomy (and were therefore areas where the Crown had less monopoly power), both areas suffered rebellions, and both suffered from internal barriers to trade. As already recounted in Chapter 7, Catalonia was not integrated into the Spanish (Castilian) economy and at times was economically discriminated against; it engaged in actual revolution in the seventeenth century. The Low Countries also revolted against the Habsburgs during the early modern period. Revolution was one means of changing governments and was a check upon absolutism. The potential revolution set the limits on absolute power.

The different resource endowments and the striking difference in the sources of tax revenue between the two countries provides the major explanation for the very diverse pattern of economic development. In France, the lack of a readily visible tax base required high initial transactions costs in creating a bureaucratic structure for direct taxation; but once created, the tax could be increased at very little additional cost within the limits of the monopoly enjoyed by the Crown. This pattern had some parallels in Spain with the *alcabala*, but of the three great sources of revenue of the Spanish Crown – the Mesta, payments from the Low Countries and other possessions, and treasure from the New World – two were external. This shaped the destiny of Spain. The external sources provided a ready and growing source of revenue, which not only explains the rise of Spanish political power and the great Habsburg empire under Charles V and Philip II, but equally explains the decline of Spanish power already evident under Philip II – decline which precipitously continued under Philip III and Philip IV as these revenue sources were lost. The Spanish Empire depended on non-Spanish revenues and waxed and waned with them.

Spain's story begins where we left off in Chapter 7. 'In the greater part of Spain around 1476 no one could say "this is mine" and "that is yours" for the luck of a battle, the favor of a sovereign, a change of sides were enough to cause a person's property to be confiscated and given to someone else. It was a state of generalized chaos. Ferdinand and Isabella re-established peace and stabilized property.'[2] The price of domestic peace and secure property rights, as we noted earlier, was loss of liberty in the Cortes, the grant to the Crown of the sole power to set taxes.

Before the Habsburgs, the Mesta, discussed above, constituted within Spain the financial backbone of the Crown. However, we are left to wonder why Ferdinand and Isabella did not follow the longer-run path of agricultural prosperity, which would have occurred had they curtailed the monopolistic privileges of the Mesta and encouraged the development of property rights in land for arable use. The answer is most concisely stated by Vives.

Therefore, instead of waiting for a few years until the development of agriculture would bear fruit, the monarchs chose to follow the easy path of their predecessors and collect money on something as tangible and easily taxable as sheep. This brings us to the second motive: *the financial*

---

[2] Vincens Vives, *Economic History of Spain*, p. 294.

crisis undergone by the Crown after 1484. Owing to the expansion of the Inquisition and the flight of capital in the hands of the *conversos*, and subsequently, in 1492, to the expulsion of the Jews, quick remedies were needed; and none was closer to hand than the wool which was exported. Hence the protection of the Mesta. Hence too, after the time of Ferdinand and Isabelle, it could be said that, 'The exploitation and preservation of sheepherding is the chief support of these kingdoms.'[3]

Charles V's ascension to the throne in 1516 marked the beginning of the great era of Spanish supremacy and hegemony over much of Europe. It was at least initially, an era of prosperity and of a vast increase in the fiscal resources of the state. The Mesta became a relatively less important source of revenue; the *alcabala* continued to be an important source of Castilian revenue, but was equalled by revenues from Aragon, Naples and Milan; but overshadowing all others were the revenues from the Low Countries, which in some years were ten times greater than any other single source, including remittances from the Indies.[4]

However, the revenues from the Spanish Empire were more than matched by the expense of maintaining and attempting to extend the empire, and Charles V resorted increasingly in times of crisis to loans. These *asientos* were guaranteed by the state's fiscal revenues. By 1562, 1,430,000 ducats or over one quarter of the annual budget had to be paid out as interest on previous loans. Increasingly the state resorted to unilateral measures: lengthening maturities, reducing interest rates, raising the price of gold and in 1557 declaring itself bankrupt. This policy was repeated in 1575, 1576, 1607, 1627 and 1647.

It is not hard to explain rising expenditures. Habsburg hegemony over much of Europe involved recurrent warfare and the largest (and best trained) army in Europe, the development of a navy and the expenses of dealing with periodic rebellions.

Charles V and Philip II were required to spend more each year to keep together the house of cards they had constructed and expenditures persistently seemed to exceed revenues. As the revenues from the Low Countries fell off with their revolt and the subsequent success of the seven northern provinces in achieving independence, the Crown was forced to squeeze the traditional sources still harder. In the last third of the sixteenth century the *alcabala* and the *millones* (a levy which required a number of taxes) increased sharply in real terms. Treasure from the New World was seized by the Crown, but when this last great external source of revenue

---

[3] *Ibid.*, p. 304.
[4] *Ibid.*; p. 382 lists revenues as follows: *alcabala*, 267,000 ducats; Aragon, 200,000 ducats; Naples 290,000 ducats; Milan, 300,000 ducats; Low Countries, 4,000,000 ducats; Indies, 350–400,000 ducats. Total: 5,407,300 ducats to 5,457,000 ducats. These are sixteenth-century figures, but no specific date is given.

levelled off at the end of the sixteenth century and then declined precipitously from the 1630s onward, the Crown was forced to more and more desperate expedients. Copper coinage was substituted for silver and the results are succinctly described by Elliott:

> Olivares tried to compensate for the disastrous drop in the purchasing power of Castilian money by raising the level of taxation in Castile and inventing a host of ingenious fiscal devices to extract money from the privileged and the exempt. In many ways he was extremely successful. The Castilian aristocracy was so intensively mulcted that a title, so far from being a badge of exemption, became a positive liability, and the Venetian ambassador who arrived in 1638 reported Olivares as saying that, if the war continued, no one need think of possessing his own money any more since everything would belong to the king. While this fiscal policy, when applied to the Castilian nobles, caused no more than impotent rumblings of discontent, it proved to be self-defeating when adopted towards what remained of the Castilian merchant community. The long series of arbitrary confiscations of American silver remittances to individual merchants in Seville, who were 'compensated' by the grant of relatively worthless juros, proved fatal to the town's commercial life. Olivares' tenure of power saw the final alienation of Spain's native business community from its king, and the final defeat of native commercial enterprise in the name of royal necessity. The crumbling of the elaborate credit structure of Seville and the collapse of Seville's trading system with the New World between 1639 and 1641, was the price that Olivares had to pay for his cavalier treatment of Spanish merchants.[5]

The consequences for efficient property rights of the Spanish Crown's fiscal policies can be very quickly summarized. In the case of agriculture, the decrees favoring the Mesta effectively thwarted the development of efficient property rights in land. The royal order of 1480, for example, ordered evacuation of enclosures set up by farmers on communal land; the Edict of 1489 redrew (widened) the boundaries of Granada's sheepwalks; the Edict of 1491 banned enclosures in Granada; and the land lease law of 1501 in effect permitted sheep to graze anywhere that they had at any time previously occupied for a few months and allowed their owners to pay in perpetuity the original rental fee; if they had grazed without the owner's knowledge they paid no rent. The development of arable agriculture was further weakened when a price ceiling was imposed on wheat in 1539. In a century of inflation the fixed rent on land and the ceiling price on wheat had predictable consequences in the celebrated depopulation of the countryside and even recurrent local famines. There were simply few incentives to engage in arable agriculture and much less to improve it. Indeed the

[5] J. H. Elliott, 'The Decline of Spain', *Past and Present*, 20 (November 1961), 71.

expulsion of the Moriscos in the early seventeenth century deprived Spain of a group skilled in irrigated agriculture. Spain's agricultural organization remained suited to a prior day.

However, the tragedy of Spain's decline and stagnation is not simply an account of depriving minorities of their property (first the Jews in 1492 and then the Moors). As the previous quotation makes clear, they were only symptomatic of the insecurity of all property rights. As the Crown's financial difficulties increased, seizure, confiscation, or the unilateral alteration of contracts were recurrent phenomena which ultimately affected every group engaged in commerce or industry as well as agriculture. As a consequence people were driven out of productive pursuits. As no property right was secure, economic retardation was the inevitable consequence. Elliott succinctly summarized the consequences: 'The nature of the economic system was such that one became a student or a monk, a beggar or a bureaucrat. There was nothing else to be.'[6]

The decline of Spain has received relatively much attention from scholars. In a sense this effort has been misspent. It is true that Spain attempted to dominate the Western World and failed, but it tried to do so with foreign revenues. Spain itself provided only about 10 percent of the empire's revenues at its height. Its economy remained medieval throughout its bid for political dominance. Where it retained political sway, as in the Spanish Netherlands, the economy of the area withered and declined. Spain provides an excellent example of the results and consequences of failing to develop an efficient economic organization.

[6] *Ibid*, p. 87. The definitive study of the Mesta is Julius Klein, *The Mesta* (Harvard University Press, 1920). See, in particular, p. 322 for a description of the law of 'possession'.

11. THE NETHERLANDS AND SUCCESSFUL ECONOMIC GROWTH

The Netherlands, in particular the seven provinces in the north, were the first areas of Western Europe to escape the Malthusian checks. The United Provinces, as we have seen, generated a sustained increase in *per capita* income during the seventeenth century, at the same time as they supported an increasing population.

It was in this area that a fortunate conjunction occurred between the interests of the state and the interests of the progressive sector of society. The Low Countries since the Middle Ages had been the natural entrepot of Western Europe and continued to enjoy this role through the seventeenth century, obtaining a practical monopoly of European transport and international commerce. This dominance, due to location, superior commercial techniques and the enormous backwardness of their neighbors, remained intact through the first quarter of the eighteenth century.

The Dutch success is all the more interesting because it was a small country with relatively few resources. Instead of relying upon nature to provide its bounty, the Dutch developed an efficient economic organization compared to their rivals and in so doing achieved an economic and political importance all out of proportion to the small size of their country.

Henri Pirenne makes clear that the Burgundian state was a truly remarkable political phenomenon, welding together the diverse and jealous cities and towns of the region.[1] Between the end of the fourteenth century and the mid-sixteenth century the four dukes of Burgundy (and after the Habsburg inheritance, Charles V) played an important role in the emergence of the area as the commercial leader of Northern Europe. In general the economic interests of these rulers lay in promoting international trade, in reducing guild exclusiveness and monopoly and in preventing the local guilds from imposing their restrictive practices on the development of industry in the country. These were precisely the policies that favored the development of an efficient economic organization. The Burgundian dukes were opposed by the old privileged towns of Bruges and Ghent, but solidly supported by the new centers of industry and commerce, which because of

[1] See Henri Pirenne, 'The Formation and Constitution of the Burgundian State', *American Historical Review*, 14, pp. 477–502.

their efficiency thrived in international competition. Their relative efficiency was due to their location and the fact that they eliminated restrictive practices and welcomed foreign merchants and financiers from southern Germany and the northern Italian cities. The rise of Antwerp during the sixteenth century to an unparalleled importance in trade and finance was not only a result of its liberal trade policies, which attracted the cloth trade and made it the entrepot for Portuguese spices and the great center of international finance, but was also due to the Burgundian dukes' support of the institutions that developed there.

Coinciding with the growth of Antwerp was the relatively unfettered development of cloth manufacture in the countryside: In contrast with the drapery trade in the towns, the cloth manufacture in the country districts entered upon a career of astonishing progress. Reduced, during the whole of the Middle Ages, to a precarious and miserable existence by the jealously guarded privileges of the towns, it had begun to expand here and there during the Burgundian period, in spite of many difficulties and constant complaints. Then suddenly, toward the end of the first third of the sixteenth century it became very prosperous. The result was the growth of a new system of industry, fundamentally different from the old corporate organization, which still existed side by side with it, and as well adapted to the new economic order as the guild system was incompatible with it. Free from all the fetters with which municipal regulation had narrowly confined the artisan, the new development answered all the requirements of capitalist enterprise. Under the new conditions there were no limits to the output, no craft uniting the artisans against the employer, interfering with the rate of wages, fixing the conditions of apprenticeship and limiting the hours of work. Above all there were no privileges restricting admission to the trade to Burghers only, and excluding 'foreigners', as all new burghers had long been styled. Here every man was sure of being employed provided he was ablebodied and knew how to throw a shuttle.[2]

The countryside also made dramatic advances in increasing the efficiency of agriculture, which we shall discuss below. In sum the developments in the Netherlands were striking in all areas. The studies made by the Low Countries in improving agricultural efficiency were more than matched by their developments in commerce, trade and industry.

In order to explain the precocious developments in all these areas we must look to the underlying institutional structures, especially the establishment and protection of private property. We have already mentioned that

---

[2] Henri Pirenne, *Early Democracy in the Low Countries* (W. W. Norton, 1963), pp. 206–7. A similar development occurred in the iron and coal industry in the provinces of Liege, Namur and Hainault.

by 1500 land and man were free of manorial obligations. Another major feature carried over from the Burgundian era was a positive encouragement mobility of productive factors. For example, foreign merchants and craftsmen with special skills were allowed to follow their trades in spite of local guild opposition. Most attempts at monopoly were discouraged. Commercial innovations that lowered transaction costs were recognized by law. Trade and commerce prospered within the context of the institutional environment that developed. The only property right encouraging economic growth that was missing was an efficient system for the protection of knowledge.

While the Burgundian dukes were encouraging a course of economic development which threatened and displeased the old privileged towns because it encouraged new and unfettered industry and commerce, they developed their political administration without displacing the provincial states-general or the town magistrates' local powers. In 1463, Philip the Good had created the States General, made up of delegates of the provincial assemblies, which passed laws and, most important, held the authority to grant taxes to the Crown.

Overall Burgundian and Habsburg policy was to promote unification and trade, which redounded to the prosperity of the economy and hence of the Crown. Throughout the wars of Charles V in the sixteenth century, the seventeen provinces remained loyal and provided increasing revenue for the conquest of the growing empire. The Low Countries had because of their prosperity become the jewels of the Habsburg Empire, furnishing the Crown with the bulk of its revenues. The very success of Burgundian and Habsburg efforts at unification ultimately provided the basis for unified opposition to them. The Habsburgs, caught in the continual warfare of this era, faced fiscal crisis after crisis and persistently sought more and more tax revenues from the Low Countries. Although the Low Countries had tolerated Charles V, they were no longer willing to put up with the more exacting demands of his successor Philip II. Accepting the leadership of the House of Orange, the Low Countries revolted and a long struggle, complicated by religious controversy, ensued. The sack of Antwerp resulted in the rise of Amsterdam and in the eventual independence of the north, which formed the Seven United Provinces. The republic that emerged under the leadership of Amsterdam carried with it the structure of law and property rights that had been fostered and developed under the Burgundian regime.

II

The growth of trade and commerce was the prime mover of the Dutch economy throughout the early modern period. The growth of European population, especially during the sixteenth century, worked to the benefit of the centrally located Netherlands. The market, or the transactions sector, which linked agriculture and industry with one another and ultimately with the consumer, was the sector where at this time large gains in productivity could occur. The transactions sector historically had been the most important in the Netherlands and was the sector from which the bulk of government revenues were directly drawn. The state, except during periods of crisis, had every incentive to provide measures that, by lowering transaction costs, stimulated commerce.

Thus, in the centrally located Low Countries, a process was set in motion whereby the growth of European population could stimulate innovations that increased the efficiency of economic organization by lowering transaction costs. The commercial innovations that were adopted during this era were not new, for most had been developed earlier by the Italians. They were, however, efficient only when they could be employed on a relatively large scale. The expanding market and, for the most part, a favorable political climate created the conditions for their profitable employment. Innovations which directly lowered the cost of using the market, new commercial organizations that facilitated the access of small merchants to profitable opportunities, and especially the establishment of a capital market, characterize this era in Dutch economic history.

The costs of using the market to organize an economy are the costs of making exchanges. These costs, as we have seen, can be broken down into search costs, negotiation costs and enforcement costs. In each of these areas the Dutch economy became more efficient.

Search costs are the costs involved in locating potential buyers or sellers with whom to negotiate trades. The markets of the Netherlands were a means of reducing search costs. There was the rise and decline of regional fairs in the Low Countries, the rise and fall of first Bruges and then Antwerp, and the final ascendance of Amsterdam; each market in its turn was larger than its predecessor. The economies of scale inherent in a market ensured that only one central place at a time could dominate. These central places served as an international market and, by their very nature, significantly reduced search costs. There buyers and sellers concentrated in larger numbers than anywhere else in Northern Europe. In these central places the range of products offered and the range of the terms of sale tendered were greater than anywhere else. The assurance of a large market allowed specialization in both products and sale conditions. Permanent sales halls or *bourses* were established. There specialized merchants continually displayed goods or samples. Previously sales halls had been available to rent only for the duration of a fair. During this period foreign commerce became a year-round occupation.

The negotiation costs involved in making a transaction can be summed up by the phrase *quid pro quo*. While the pure price of an exchange is obviously the central variable, there are many other elements involved in a transaction. The quality of the good to be exchanged must be agreed upon, as well as the place and time at which the exchange will occur. Also it must be determined how, when and in what form, payment will be made. These non-price elements are important in any bargain. Buyers and sellers must agree on all of these elements in a transaction before a trading contract is made. Since a large number of buyers and sellers were concentrated in the markets of the Low Countries, the chance of negotiating a favorable exchange was greater there than elsewhere. From the large volume of transactions which daily took place standard operating practices evolved. Because they lowered negotiating costs, customary terms of sale, sanctioned by law, were applied to much of this trade or, at the very least, offered a starting point from which particular bargains could be negotiated.

The large continuous volume of transactions in a particular commodity made it possible to begin to sell by sample. A London merchant, for example, could purchase grain from the Baltic in these markets, seeing and retaining only a sample. The seller warranted that the delivered goods would be as good or better than the sample. Sales according to grade and the growth of future markets were a direct extension of this practice. Grains, wine, wood and wool could be sold even before they were harvested.

Enforcement costs, the costs of ensuring that the terms of the trading contract were met as negotiated, were also reduced through time. Customary trading practices were sanctioned by the government. Should any of the conditions of a contract be violated, the merchant who had suffered could sue for adjustment in the law courts near the market. A decision by such a court could not be ignored if the offending merchant desired to continue to operate in the most efficient market in Western Europe. Public notaries established their offices near the marketplaces, where they witnessed and recorded contracts and mediated in commercial disputes. Notaries thus replaced local magistrates in performing this function, increasing by specialization the efficiency with which contracts were enforced.

The growth of the market to a size sufficiently large to allow the customary contracted terms of sale for a product of known quality to account for a large number of transactions was extremely important. It allowed a freely obtained market price to be determined by the forces of supply and demand alone. Beginning in the last quarter of the sixteenth century these prices were periodically gathered and printed. The Amsterdam 'price current' was widely circulated and provided information about the terms at which exchanges could be made. These price currents have been found in the archives of every important European city. They provided a merchant with a starting point to negotiate trades in local areas both in the Low Countries and outside. No merchant would sell locally for less than he could obtain in Amsterdam, making allowance for the costs of moving his goods there.

The expansion of international commerce during the sixteenth and seventeenth centuries was also aided by the significant decline in the costs of transporting goods. The costs of both overland and sea transport declined, thereby allowing a growing commerce in lower-value bulky commodities. In this development maritime commerce took the lead. The Mediterranean, the Baltic and the lands of Africa, Asia and the New World were linked by sea traders. Inland trade routes and fairs, which still grew absolutely, declined relative to the peripheries adjoining the sea. The expanding great markets of the sixteenth and seventeenth centuries were connected to each other via navigable bodies of water.

The small sea-going vessels of the early sixteenth century were well adapted to the restricted maritime trade of the early modern era. Many seaports, such as Antwerp, Rouen, London and Seville, were situated on the estuaries of rivers quite a way inland. They were accessible only to ships of small draft. When trade is not extensive, small ships have the decided advantage of quicker turn-around times. The presence of French, English and Dutch pirates also made it advantageous to divide a merchant's cargoes between several ships, thus reducing the risk of total loss.

After 1500 the development of specialized trades, such as the Baltic timber trade, made larger ships economical. The elimination or reduction of piracy, the expansion in the number of international cargoes and the development of maritime insurance all combined to make larger ships more economical on route after route. The average tonnage of vessels increased slowly. As a consequence of all these developments productivity in ocean shipping increased at a rate of between $\frac{1}{2}$ and 1 percent *per annum* between 1600 and 1750, increasing the efficiency of trade in the process.

The increase in productivity in the shipping industry was in large part due to the spread of an innovation. The development of a new cargo-carrying sailing ship called the flute was a major advance, which represented a clear break from the combination military vessels and cargo carriers of earlier times. It was developed by the Dutch in approximately 1595, but its introduction into the various commodity routes of the world was determined by the growth of large-scale, regular, efficient markets between trading areas and the elimination of piracy and privateering on the shipping lanes. The flute sacrificed reinforced construction (which could support both the weight and recoil of cannons as well as the weight of other armaments and of complex rigging) for cargo space and simplicity of handling, which allowed smaller crew size. The result was apparent in dramatically lower direct costs of operation. Such a ship was immediately practical in the Baltic, where a large-scale regular trade existed and piracy and privateering had been eliminated. But since the ship was designed for the bulk carriage of commodities in large volume and was relatively defenseless, the likelihood of under-utilization and the costs of protection (or of insurance) on routes such as the pirate-infested Mediterranean vitiated these cost savings. The introduction of ships of this general type was delayed on routes such as this until regular markets had been developed and piracy reduced or eliminated.

Market areas located inland were not ignored. Certain firms specialized in overland trade and by concentrated effort reduced the risks of travel. Caravans or land convoys protected goods in transit. This allowed the small merchant to participate in long-distance overland trade. The famous Hesse carts of Germany and the large Italian firms whose purpose was to maintain and protect overland trade routes are good examples.

Changes in commercial organization during these centuries were generally not characterized by new inventions, but by the innovation of known techniques discovered earlier by the Italians. The rapid expansion of the market in the Low Countries made it possible to develop new arrangements that would have been inefficient at lower levels of business activity.

The new element in commercial organization during these two centuries lay in the innovation of more flexible methods for the communal exploitation of profitable commercial opportunities than were possessed by the earlier great centralized German and Italian family companies. The share company and the commission merchant are good and important examples. The pooling of capital in the form of shares in a temporary association, for example, allowed a number of small merchants to furnish the large amounts of capital necessary to finance distant ocean voyages and permitted the considerable risks involved to be shared. The use of a fellow merchant situated in another market to buy or sell for a fixed commission also allowed small merchants to participate in commerce outside their local markets. These organizational techniques furnished the small merchant with the tools needed to participate in large ventures and in transcontinental trade. While, in the main, merchants remained organized as family businesses or small partnerships, their methods became more sophisticated. Not only were they better informed about trading possibilities, but they were more adept at exploiting them. The human capital of the merchants was strikingly upgraded during the period. Formal business schooling became an accepted practice. The techniques of double entry book-keeping were widely taught and became the standard accounting practice.

III

The development of a capital market during this period was inseparable from the rise of commerce and the continual conflict between the major nation-states. The crowns of Europe had become borrowers in times of crisis as soon as any group became prosperous enough to be lenders on a sufficiently large scale. Merchants seeking concessions were a prime source of loans and vulnerable to the point where they were a group from which to extract forced loans. We have seen in previous chapters that the large Italian and German family firms became lenders to kings, receiving in return commissions, mineral leases, monopolies and/or the right to collect taxes. Eventually, perhaps without exception, the princes of these merchants ruined their creditors by defaulting or outright confiscation. It was difficult to sue a king.

The fiscal needs of government created one element of the demand for loans and the growing specialization of the international and regional economies another. Capital is generally considered to be a factor of production that has a life longer than one year. Capital affords the manufacturer a more specialized round-about production process, allowing gains from the division of labor to be achieved or complementary production processes of different time spans to be joined together. The essence of capital is time, and both government and individual economic units can gain in various ways if they can obtain resources now and pay later. The less they have to pay later, the more they will want to borrow today. There are also persons who are willing to give up some of their current resources in return for the future repayment plus a premium (interest). The higher the interest, the more they are willing to lend. Thus a situation exists in which both groups can gain from trade.

A capital market brings together the potential borrowers and lenders for purposes of making such a trade. The creation of a loan, like any voluntary transaction, while it benefits both parties, requires resources. There are search costs as potential borrowers and lenders seek to contact each other. There are also negotiation costs as both parties seek to reach agreement about what is borrowed, where, and for what price and, especially important for loans, what guarantees are to be given to ensure repayment. A loan, unlike the direct purchase of wheat, takes place on two separate dates: the granting of the loan and, in time, its repayment. There are also enforcement costs to ensure that all the conditions of the contract are met. Thus there are as many variables in the creation of a loan as in any other transaction.

The more efficient the market the lower the search, negotiation and enforcement costs of creating loans. A capital market is a money market: money is borrowed, used for whatever purpose and returned with interest. The natural place for a capital market to develop in Western Europe was at the center of commerce. A European capital market developed first at the regional fairs, then at Bruges, then at Antwerp and finally shifted with commerce to Amsterdam. During the early sixteenth century, the exchange at Antwerp dominated Europe's transactions in bills of exchange and other credit instruments, such as demand notes, deposit certificates and the bonds of states and towns. This exchange at one time had 5000 members. Goods were traded elsewhere in the city, while the Exchange specialized in credit instruments. During the next century the money market in Amsterdam was even larger.

The development of an efficient capital market had been hindered since lending at interest had been prohibited by Pope Clement V in 1312. This ban, of course, was not effective, but neither was it directly defied. Instead, surreptitious means of circumventing it were required; false leases instead of mortgages and silent partners instead of direct loans are examples. This necessity raised the search, negotiation and especially the enforcement costs and reduced the availability of credit. Even during the Reformation the ethics of charging interest and the general question of usury were still debated. But the young nation-states needed a capital market. Finally, in 1543, Charles V approved lending at interest. Elsewhere, too, the acquisitive spirit triumphed over moral qualms and lending at interest became acceptable, making possible the development of an efficient capital market in Western Europe.

The capital market that developed in Antwerp and Amsterdam was as complex as the product markets. It is perhaps best to divide the capital market arbitrarily in two, so that we can first trace the development of short-term credit, which was closely associated with loans for commercial purposes, and then the long-term capital market, which was associated with loans to governments.

The creation of a short-term capital market was facilitated by the acceptance of two means of deferred payment. The letter obligatory was a means of deferring payment until a future date. The amount, the date, and the place was specified. It was similar to an I.O.U.

Increasingly in the place of the 'U' was written the phrase 'payable to bearer'. Thus an individual could give the note to someone else in payment of a debt and he or his assigns could collect the money owed whenever it fell due. This was called an assignment and was an important development, because it allowed another possible means of payment. In order to allow the widespread use of assignments, it was necessary to establish the legal right of endorsement. This required that the law recognize that the individual endorsing the note was still responsible for the debt for which he assigned someone else's I.O.U. in payment until the note was paid. This ensured that if the letters obligatory were defaulted the endorser was still responsible for the debt. Without this elementary guarantee, few people would accept as a payment from one individual someone else's note.

By 1507 the Antwerp *turba* (the *turba* was a group of citizens who made sworn statements on the state of legal custom for a certain area) had already decided that endorsement was the custom. Soon after, this practice also prevailed in other areas of the Low Countries. In 1537 it became law for the whole of the Netherlands. Thereafter the principle of assignment was enforced by the state. It was a natural step for merchants to begin to discount such notes. If a merchant holding notes due in the future decided he needed cash now, he could sell them to another not so pressed, for a sum less than the face value. The merchant thus obtained cash and the buyer earned the difference between what he paid for the bill and its face value.

The assignment principle was also used in bills of exchange. A bill of exchange allowed, for example, the purchase of goods in London, with the final payment to be made in a foreign currency in another country, say in Amsterdam. Needless to say, the acceptance of a letter obligatory or a bill of exchange depended upon the reputation of the maker of the note. If the maker were a large merchant, like a Fugger, there would be little doubt that it was good. Thus a practice arose whereby smaller merchants maintained deposits with larger firms upon which they could draw bills of exchange.

Eventually deposit banking developed out of this practice. In the case of the exchange bank of Amsterdam, the deposits were ultimately guaranteed by the government itself, and while the deposits paid no interest they were safe, which was no small advantage in times of turmoil.

The means of payment available to merchants thus expanded from barter or cash to include deferred payments. Merchants now had a new tool with which to extend their business. It has been stated by a historian of the subject that the technical equipment of Dutch merchants developed during the sixteenth century 'had become so refined and rational that the element of risk tended to be more and more to the effect of natural phenomena such as weather and seasons'.[3] While this is perhaps an exaggeration, it is clear that in the Netherlands property rights appropriate for the development of both an efficient product market and a short-term capital market had been created. The influence of those developments, as we shall see, permeated the entire Dutch economy.

The long-term capital stemmed from and was dominated by loans to states. Charles V, for example, became Europe's largest debtor. The Fuggers were the Spanish Crown's largest creditors. During this period it became impossible to distinguish sharply between the loans to the Spanish Crown and the credit of the Spanish Netherlands, since the Crown forced the cities and government to borrow for it. Much of the borrowing was done on the Antwerp exchange. The subsequent six bankruptcies of the Spanish Crown in 1557, 1575, 1596, 1607, 1627 and 1647 wiped out the Fuggers and severely damaged the long-term credit market. Nevertheless,

[3] Herman Van der Wee, *The Growth of the Antwerp Market and the European Economy* (Martinus Nijhoff, 1963), vol. 2, p. 295.

the advantages to both borrowers and lenders from loaning money for long periods were too great for the practice to be eliminated by such spectacular reverses.

All the heads of state borrowed during these centuries to meet continual emergencies and fiscal crises. One form of borrowing was the perpetual annuity, the payment of interest annually forever for the loan of a sum of money. During desperate times, coercion was often resorted to and forced loans obtained in this manner. Such procedures were, however, self-defeating in the end. During the seventeenth century, because of state policy, the markets for long-term loans became national in character. Now free from Spanish domination, Amsterdam, by the use of sound fiscal practices, created such an efficient long-term capital market that the rate of interest fell to as low as 3 percent. The interest rate was higher elsewhere in direct proportion to the fiscal position, the efficiency of the market and reputation of the governments.

The efficiency of the Dutch capital market lay in its initial centralization as the money market for Western Europe. The fact that foreign commerce was centralized there allowed the creation and extension of a European capital market. Search costs were reduced and fundamental and secondary institutions were created that lowered transaction costs.

The development of an efficient capital market in the Low Countries had tremendous implications for the functioning of commerce and industry. The capital market consisted of a host of intermediaries bringing together borrowers and lenders. The intermediaries, armed with the new financial devices, became so efficient that the rate of interest was drastically reduced, from 20–30 percent in 1500 to 9–12 percent in 1550 and to 3 percent or even less during the seventeenth century. Thus the cost of capital fell substantially relative to the prices of the other factors of production. No sector of the economy of the Netherlands was immune from the influence of this dramatic change in relative factor prices. Capital, financial and physical, was increasingly substituted for other productive factors in agriculture and industry as well as commerce.

IV

Agriculture became more capital-intensive, wastes were drained and cleared, fencing was improved and fertilizers were extensively employed. Credit was increasingly utilized to finance all business activity and more roundabout, specialized means of production were employed. Industrial production became at once larger in scope and more specialized.

In a previous chapter we noted the early development of private property in land and the emergence of a free labor force in the Low Countries. It is perhaps worth briefly summarizing these developments. Serfdom, where it had existed, had disappeared in most parts of Flanders and Brabant in the course of the twelfth and thirteenth centuries. The rise of the market, typified by Bruges, made vassalage inefficient. In the process the manors had been carved up into small peasant holdings. These developments, coupled with the effect of diminishing returns to a growing labor force on the value of land, made the extension of cultivation profitable. The extension of agricultural land in this area depended upon the possibilities of reclamation from the sea. Polder-making required, besides large capital investments, the guarantee that the investor alone would reap most of the benefits. Thus private property in land, the most efficient means of doing this, was incorporated into the fundamental institutional arrangements of the area.

The general decline in population during the fourteenth and fifteenth centuries eliminated the incentive to reclaim land. The Dutch countryside during the fifteenth century lost one-third of its inhabitants to war and famine. The land lost to floods during this era was often not even reclaimed. Nevertheless, the small peasant owner – operator, with 7 to 10 acres, continued to dominate the organization of agriculture.

The revival of population growth everywhere in Europe during the sixteenth century and the stimulus to trade and commerce induced new developments in Dutch agriculture. These developments were in general not due to new technology but to the profits inherent in adjusting crops and processes to new market conditions. The owner–operators of the small farms, free from the restrictions of common fields, could adjust quickly to changes in market demand and, since the proprietors alone captured the inherent rewards, had every incentive to do so.

The rise of the international market led to regional specialization. Vineyards, for example, disappeared from Brabant, beekeeping declined and dairying moved to the North. These crops were replaced by the growing of cole seed, hays, madder, tobacco, flax, hops and quality grains for the manufacture of beer. The arable land was more intensely utilized and thus required more manure; hence more animals were needed. New crop rotations were introduced to maintain fertility. The fallow was turned into arable to grow fodder crops for wintering animals. So specialized had agriculture become and so far had the market penetrated the organization of agriculture that a market developed for manure to be used as fertilizer.

The widespread introduction of fodder and industrial crops was possible only because the commercial markets of the Low Countries had become efficient enough to allow importation of foodstuffs to feed the large urban population.

The free laborer of the countryside, given the existence of private property in land, had every incentive to employ his resources for his own benefit, which was in this case also in the interests of society. The fundamental institutions in Dutch agriculture, private property, a free labor force and a market, were consistent with economic growth. The opportunities for this growth were provided during this era by the growth of the market. The fundamental institutional organization allowed the Dutch farmer to make rapid adjustments to changes in product and factor prices. The Dutch as a result became the pioneers in new agricultural methods; methods derived from specialization and efficient resource allocations, not invention.

This is not to suggest that technological progress was absent; it was not. A specialized sickle was developed, for example. The gains that were made in this area, however, can also be accounted for by the expansion of the commercial sector. They were without exception improvements, like the technological developments of the Middle Ages, which derived from the focusing of men's minds on more specialized areas and required few private resources to develop. A method of guaranteeing the gains of new knowledge to the inventor was still absent from the fundamental institutional situation.

V

We have seen that the Low Countries were the first important center of Western European manufacturing. This was particularly true of the textile industry. The growth of efficient markets allowed the easy importation of raw materials and facilitated the sale of the final product for export. Cloth was manufactured under the regulations of highly specialized guilds. The fortunes of the industrial sector and of the area in general were dependent upon the Malthusian cycle. When population in Europe grew, so did trade and manufacturing; when population fell, commerce and industry also declined. During the population trough of the fifteenth century, English cloth became a prime competitor. In response, the urban centers of the Netherlands began to specialize in luxury and semi-luxury textiles.

Rural industry in the Low Countries remained of limited importance until 1500. Thereafter, as trade and commerce expanded throughout Europe, rural manufacture became of increasing importance. The production of inexpensive linens and light woolens was concentrated in the countryside. The rise of commercial activity, the development of an efficient capital market and the policy of the government made this possible. The reduction in the cost of capital allowed the use of more capital in the manufacturing process; the absence of guild regulations in the country allowed the manufacturing process to be free of restrictive guild practices and to employ less expensive rural labor. The conditions allowed the relatively densely settled Dutch countryside to develop according to its comparative advantage.

The growth of the international market caused the craft guilds of the cities to specialize increasingly in the production of luxury and semi-luxury goods. Meanwhile in the countryside a textile industry developed concentrating on less expensive cloths under a putting-out system, directed by urban merchants. The merchant granted the weaver raw materials or monies, giving instructions on processing and then, at a specified time in the future, took delivery of the goods. While the craft guilds objected to this turn of events, the political power of the commercial sector dominated governmental policy. Encouraging rural industry, which they organized and financed, was in the interest of the powerful merchants. Thus the restrictive practices of the guilds were themselves restricted to the towns. In the country, the free sway of market forces dominated.

The Dutch during the early modern period became the economic leaders of Europe. Their centrally located geographical position and their government, which established an efficient economic organization, account for this growth. Economic historians have sometimes dismissed the Dutch as the last great city-state or even confused their relative decline with absolute decline. In point of fact the Netherlands was the first country to achieve sustained economic growth in the sense we have defined it. Moreover, far from declining, they continue to thrive and achieve higher levels of *per capita* income in successive decades and even centuries. It is simply that the center of the economic stage shifts to England.

12. ENGLAND

The size of France and the financial resources of Spain made those countries powers in Europe. The efficiency of the Netherlands achieved the same thing. All three presented England with a continual challenge, since she lacked the size of France, the foreign endowments of Spain and the efficient institutions of the United Provinces. England had to seek a middle ground. Early in the seventeenth century she began to construct a New World empire in defiance of Spain. During the course of the century, England attempted to quarantine the Dutch on the one hand and to imitate the property rights and institutional arrangements of the Netherlands on the other. By 1700 England had succeeded, and early in the next century supplanted the Dutch as the most efficient and rapidly growing nation in the world.

I

However, there was little indication during the sixteenth century that England would follow the path to successful economic growth. England during the fourteenth and fifteenth centuries had also undergone the travail associated with the reduction in the powers of the barons. The country had engaged in the Hundred Years War and suffered the War of the Roses with the attendant disorders, rebellions and maladministration of justice. Yet Henry Tudor's victory at Bosworth Field in 1485 did not bring the Tudor dynasty the absolute control over the power to tax that was achieved in similar circumstances by the Crowns of France and Spain.

With the Tudors, the English monarchy was at the zenith of its powers. Still, during the era of rising nation-states, Henry VII was confronted with the restriction that the king was expected to 'live on his own'. This king did manage to expand his revenues to meet the requirements of state-building in ingenious ways: by selling grants and privileges and by exacting an increasing number of fines and levies to augment his regular revenue sources. His successor, Henry VIII, added to his revenues by the confiscation of church lands. Yet the fact of the matter was that 'the most powerful dynasty ever to sit on England's throne was powerful only as long as it did not go outside the limits laid down by a nation'.[1] The confiscation of the monasteries' lands and possessions evidently did not extend beyond these bounds, but the king found that 'with nearly half the peers and at least four-fifths of the clergy against him, Henry had need of the House of Commons and he cultivated it with sedulous care'.[2] The rise of the House of Commons, which was dominated by the rising merchant class and landed gentry, was an integral part of Tudor political policy. This dynasty found it necessary to attempt to control parliament rather than to supplant it. The Tudors cannot be considered as other than as opportunistic in their dealing with property rights. They opposed enclosures, espoused monopolies and failed to recognize the gains that were available in extending the market. They sought revenues where they could, without regard to their effect upon economic efficiency.

The Stuarts inherited what the Tudors had sown. The Commons, by the beginning of the Stuart reign, was ready and able to assert itself. The controversy between the Stuarts and parliament is a familiar one. Its importance for our account is that in essence it was a dispute over fiscal matters.[3] The Crown, caught up in the expensive rivalry between nations, needed more revenues and parliament proved intractable. The Crown viewed the government as its prerogative, the parliament saw the Crown as circumscribed by the common law.

The early seventeenth-century history of English government is inextricably entwined with the life of Sir Edward Coke. It was Coke who insisted that common law was the supreme law of the land and repeatedly incurred the anger of James I; it was Coke who led the parliamentary opposition in the 1620s; this group was responsible for securing the common-law control over the development of commercial law; and finally his leadership of the parliamentary opposition cemented the alliance of parliament with the common law.

Coke's contribution was not confined simply to advocacy of the supremacy of the common law; he also insisted that this law should strike down those monopolistic special privileges associated with Crown prerogative. The right of the Crown to grant special privileges for the creation of markets and fairs had been exercised since the high Middle Ages. In 1331, one John Kemp, a Flemish weaver, was given a patent to undertake weaving, granting a protected market and exemption from the legal apprenticeship

[1] W. C. Richardson, *Tudor Chamber Administration* (University of Louisiana Press, 1952), p. 5.

[2] G. R. Elton, *The Tudor Revolution in Government* (Cambridge University Press, 1953), p. 4.

[3] There is no room here to trace the background of the fiscal crises which would certainly go back to Elizabeth's war expenditures, the declining revenues of 'fifteenths and tenths' in the seventeenth century, the forced levies, the crises of farming the customs and the division within the city of London. The classic source is F. C. Dietz, *English Public Finance, 1558–1641* (The Century Co., 1932).

requirements. The social justification for a patent monopoly was that a skill should be new to the country and that there should be sufficient uncertainty about techniques and markets to require that, for success, the innovator be initially free from competitors. It became increasingly clear during the last half of the sixteenth century that the Crown was using such grants as court currency either to raise money or to reward court favorites. These awards cost the Crown nothing, but the wider effects were often harmful when they interfered with existing manufactures or blocked profitable expansion.

In his writings, Coke not only attacked the Crown's grants of monopolies but also the existence of exclusive trading privileges. He regarded the Monopolies Act as a reaffirmation of the law rather than an innovation. Coke described the case of *Darcy* v. *Allein*, in which a patent monopoly of playing cards granted by the Crown was challenged (and the holder of the exclusive franchise unsuccessfully sought court action against the infringer of the patent), as a classic case of monopoly, which should be and was eliminated, the common law temporarily triumphing over the Crown.

Yet it would distort the picture to give undue prominence to an individual in describing the growth of market freedom in England. Coke mirrored the sentiments of a growing and powerful group of merchants and traders, who were restive at the restrictions imposed on their actions. The profitable opportunities in trade and commerce seemed everywhere circumscribed by privileges, barriers to entry and mobility, which had only to be removed to increase the scope and profitability of enterprise and consequently to promote economic growth. The Statute of Monopolies in 1624 did more than proscribe royal monopolies, it also embodied in the law a patent system to encourage any true innovation.

Yet the detailed political history of the first forty-one years of the seventeenth century, like that of the sixteenth century, provides, aside from the Statute of Monopolies, little indication that a set of impersonal and efficient property rights was emerging. Rather it is a piecemeal story of the Stuart's fiscal crises and their efforts to recoup their fortunes by desperate measures. There was the disastrous Cockayne scheme in 1614, whose projectors promised James I £300,000 from reorganizing the cloth trade. A series of patents were granted to overcome the smallness of fiscal revenues in the early 1620s, and the tariff and monopoly privileges were the means by which Charles I attempted to meet his deficits in the 1630s.

The consequence of these policies for the economy was not only disruption of external trade in the face of efficient Dutch competition, but the arbitrary granting of property rights internally, which increased uncertainty. In this context, Coke and his successors reacted by attempting to place the creation of property rights beyond the royal whim; to embed existing property rights in a body of impersonal law guarded by the courts.

The puritan revolution was the violent outcome of the struggle between the Crown and parliament and the consequences are familiar. After the Restoration, no serious attempt was ever again made to run the country without parliament, and after 1688 the changeover was complete – parliament was dominant. The key to the story, which contrasts so sharply with the case of France, which we have examined, was the inability of the Crown successfully to enlarge fiscal revenues through effective control of the economy. Success would have required a large bureaucracy which owed its loyalty to the king, the effective ability of the guilds to control apprenticeship and industrial regulation, and a court system responsible to royal control. All of these elements essential to success were missing in England.

The rapid rise in population during the sixteenth century, through diminishing returns in agriculture, significantly reduced the standard of living of the vast majority of Englishmen. Besides reducing real wages, as we have seen, it reversed the pattern of prices that had characterized the previous two centuries. While all goods rose in price, the price of land rose significantly relative to wages, as did the price of agricultural goods relative to industrial products. Especially the price of wool and the profits of sheep raising were enhanced by the rapid expansion in international trade. The combination of these new relative values was to create powerful incentives to readjust the allocation of resources. The policies of the Tudors were to freeze the economy, to hinder the readjustment and to maintain the *status quo*. The expansion of international trade within Europe and on the fringes created profitable if risky commercial opportunities. The Tudors favored this development with the grant of monopolies to joint stock companies. These associations, similar to those in Holland, combined limited liability with the rights to use coercion to exclude other Englishmen. While meeting with mixed success, they demonstrated the potential profitability of expanded foreign commerce.

The decline in the value of labor and the rise in the value of all European natural resources raised the benefits to be obtained by colonizing the New World. There, resources were abundant and labor scarce. The reductions in the cost of ocean transport that were occurring reduced the transport costs that New World goods must bear. So strong was the lure of New World resources that by 1640 the English had established fourteen permanent settlements in the Americas. By 1700 over half a million Englishmen lived abroad, producing a wide range of plantation crops for the mother country.

The Dutch, with the most efficient market in Europe and the cheapest ocean transport, were dangerous rivals to England in dealing with her own colonies. The English attempted to exclude the Dutch from English colonies by a series of Navigation Acts. By 1700, after having fought three wars over the issue, they had succeeded and the entire colonial market was in English hands. London grew apace in the wake of the expanding commerce, both foreign and domestic. Outports such as Bristol and Liverpool were beginning their commercial rise.

The gains to be made from extending the market created the political dissension that marked the seventeenth century. The example of the Netherlands was foremost in the minds of the rising commercial class. The private interests of these groups were at this time also basically the same as those of society as a whole, for we have seen in the case of the Netherlands that it was in the transaction sector that great gains could be made. The English during the last half of the seventeenth century made great strides in exploiting these gains. The establishment after the 1640s of a central government that was favorably disposed to the extension of commerce aided this development.

The reduced cost of using the market was the main source of productivity gains, as it had been in the Netherlands. It was the reduction of transaction costs that allowed England during the seventeenth century to support an increased population and at the same time to increase their standard of living. As the market grew, commercial innovations familiar to the Dutch were adopted by the English. Technological change both in industry and agriculture was generally absent during this era. The productivity gains that occurred were in response to the changing product and factor prices of the era, to the ability of the economy to adjust and to the decline in transaction costs, not to new knowledge.

III

In the Tudor era the major agricultural issue centered around rising wool prices. England was shifting from being a raw wool exporter to the manufacture and export of cloth. As the price of wool rose the gains from devising ways to control overgrazing of pastoral land increased. Such attempts are evidenced in increasing protests against violations of stinting arrangements (stinting being a voluntary agreement to limit the number of grazing animals), and efforts to enclose the pastoral as well as marginal arable lands. However, the costs of enforcing these agreements were high.

The enclosure of pastoral land had precedent in common law as far back as the Statute of Merton (1236), permitting the enclosure of commons. Population density in the sheep country was much less than in areas characterized by arable farming, so that the costs of obtaining agreement among the parties involved were lower. Without altering the existing fundamental institutions, stinting represented an advance in capturing some of the potential rent, although, as noted above, enforcement costs were high. Finally, a major element in the cost of enclosure was Tudor opposition. Where enclosure involved significant redistribution of wealth it led to widespread rioting and even open rebellion. The Tudor policy was mainly directed at enclosures, which resulted in taking land out of cultivation; therefore much pasture land was enclosed in the sixteenth century.

The relative rise of wool prices in the sixteenth century did not continue into the seventeenth and therefore the incentive to shift cultivated land to pasture declined. The organization of the arable land was still characterized by open field farming. The relative rise in the value of cultivated crops in the seventeenth century encouraged the introduction of new crops from America, and in particular from the more intensive agriculture of the Low Countries. Fallow, for example, could be reduced or eliminated and the supply of feed for livestock could be significantly increased by the planting of two new legumes: sanfoin and clover. Dutch immigrants introduced the turnip to Norwich soon after 1565. The new crops required elaborate agreements amongst open-field farmers planting in strips. Common pasture rights had of necessity to be restricted and innumerable half-way measures developed to capture the gains from these crops. These agreements were necessary because the pattern of property rights in land fell short of exclusive ownership. The first issue to be settled was who was entitled to use the manor's land. Then a decision had to be made about how it would be used. Thus a series of successive approximations toward exclusive property rights developed in cultivated areas. These agreements, and indeed enclosure itself, were encouraged by a gradual reversal of government policy as the Stuarts ceased to oppose enclosures. The great agricultural revolution in England is typically dated in the eighteenth century, but by the end of the seventeenth century enclosures and various types of voluntary agreements had set the scene by eliminating many of the common property aspects of land ownership and increasing the return to the cultivator from using more efficient techniques.

IV

When we turn to the non-agricultural sector we must go back in time and explore the relationship between the state and the private sector during the Tudor and Stuart eras. As Hecksher and Nef have pointed out, the difference between England and France was not in intent or even regulation 'on the books'; the difference was in enforcement and in the relative power of the Crown to act independently. Therefore, the central thread of our story goes back to the relationship between the Crown, parliament and the judicial system, discussed at the beginning of this chapter. Elizabeth's famous Statute of Artifices of 1563 provided a comprehensive codification of many medieval laws that had their origins in statutes aimed at preventing rising wages in the era following the Black Death. This statute fixed wages, provided for uniform rules for the training of apprentices and required handicraftsmen and artisans to assist at harvesting in time of need. Much additional legislation placed supervision in the hands of the guilds.

Yet the efforts of the Tudors to develop a comprehensive system of industrial regulation to 'freeze' the structure of economic activity and prevent mobility of productive factors proved ineffective. They proved inefficient because (1) the statute only covered existing industries, so that new industries escaped the apprenticeship rules; (2) despite opposition by town guilds, industry moved to the countryside and effectively escaped guild control; (3) in rapidly expanding industries, even those in existence in 1563, the pressing need for more labor led employees to ignore the regulations; (4) enforcement in the countryside was typically in the hands of unpaid Justices of the Peace, who had little incentive to enforce laws that were locally unpopular. Indeed since they were responsive to local interests, they had a positive incentive not to enforce such laws. The developments within the manufacturing sector imitated to a large extent prior developments in the Netherlands. Cloth continued to dominate in value the industrial sector. The manufacture of cloth increasingly moved to the countryside to escape guild regulations. As late as the 1530s and 1550s the guilds succeeded in obtaining legislation hindering rural clothiers. These regulations, for reasons given above, could not be enforced.

The scale of operations in heavy industry increased substantially during this period. Especially in coal-mining, tin- and lead-mining and the manufacture of iron the typical economic unit became larger. The major growth in productive capacity occurred as a result of changes in relative factor and product prices or the introduction of new industries. The rise of the coal industry, for example, was intimately associated with the rapid rise in the price of wood as the forests disappeared.

Industrial production in England became specialized geographically during the course of the seventeenth century as the market grew in extent. Most of the gains from this sector were the result of specialization. Technological change remained of minor importance. The gains made in industry, like those in agriculture, were due to the achievement of a more efficient set of property rights in both factor and product markets.

V

The Statute of Monopolies, which ended the Crown's prerogative in creating monopolies, was much more historically than a mere check to the power of the king. The granting of patents to royal favorites or to replenish the depleted fortunes of some of the English nobility has obscured the larger picture of the role of patents in developing a system of property rights instrumental in encouraging invention and innovation and its spread (particularly from the continent to England). Let us consider the implications in more detail.

England possessed a number of important advantages in the early development of property rights and their application to innovation. It had a degree of centralized political power and authority which made possible the exploitation of a potentially large market area. However, it is important to emphasize that the first 150 years of this period were not an era of competitive product markets, to look on the patents as grants of monopoly privilege that replaced competition is to miss the point. The many small local markets were everywhere (except in the Netherlands) protected against intrusion by special privilege. The fairs and markets were set up by royal grants. Merchant guilds had exclusive rights within towns, and still later craft guilds developed alongside them or replaced them. In total they reflect a hodge-podge of local markets dominated or controlled by monopoly privileges. In a society of local markets and of exclusive franchises and privileges, the ability of individuals or voluntary groups to penetrate with innovations or improvements was limited if not entirely absent. Only the collusive efforts of individuals with the Crown could achieve the coercive power to make changes within such product markets. In this context the granting of exclusive privileges by the Crown, either for commercial ventures overseas such as the merchant adventures and the East India Company, or for attracting foreigners to England who would bring new manufacturing processes with them, was a crucial part of the internalization of externalities, which by raising the potential rate of return upon activities made them worthwhile.

Early encouragement and protection, as we saw above, was given in 1331 to John Kemp, a Flemish weaver, to come to England with his servants and apprentices, and to other members of the Weaver's Mystery. The franchise given them to undertake weaving not only protected them in the English market but also bypassed the stringent laws which forbade working without a regular apprenticeship having been served. In other words, the grant provided them with a product market and protected them from the imperfections of the factor market as well. Royal authority was subsequently granted to other cloth makers to establish their manufactures in other parts of England. This policy of encouraging foreigners to bring in new innovations from the Continent was extended to many other areas: mining, metal working, silk manufacturing, ribbon weaving, etc. Of the fifty-five grants of monopoly privilege made under Elizabeth, twenty-one were issued to aliens or naturalized subjects. These included privileges for making such products as soap, machines for dredging and draining land, ovens and furnaces, oils, leather, grinding machines, salt, glass, drinking glasses, force pumps for raising water and writing paper; as well as for introducing processes for tempering iron, milling corn, extracting oil from rape seed and dressing, dyeing and calendering cloth.

It is clear, however, that by the end of Elizabeth's reign a changing benefit–cost pattern of economic activity was emerging from the widening of domestic markets, the growth of voluntary organization in the form of the joint stock company (which spread risk and reduced the imperfections of the capital market), and the growing cost of the coercive aspects of patent monopolies, in the form of blocking entry of voluntary groups to these growing markets. The seventeenth century bore witness to such a transformation. The celebrated case of *Darcy* v. *Allein* reflected the efforts of voluntary groups to break one of the more flagrant Elizabethan monopolies. But it was the Statute of Monopolies which not only reflected the fundamental change in organization between Crown monopoly and voluntary group organization, but institutionalized the internalization of the benefits from innovation, so that they became a part of the legal system of the society. In effect the rewards of innovating were no longer subject to royal favor, but were guaranteed by a set of property rights embedded in the common law. The subsequent political upheavals of the seventeenth century led to a political structure which further reinforced the property rights of voluntary groups, internalizing the gains from economic activity in a society where factor and product markets now were sufficiently developed to favor this expansion.

It is important to understand the difference between the rate of innovative activity which will occur in the absence of the ability to capture externalities and the rate that will occur if these externalities can be internalized. Innovation could and did occur historically, as we have seen, in a world when no property rights protected the innovator. However, only that kind of innovation occurred in which the costs (or risks of losses) were so small that the private rate of return exceeded them. Any innovation involving substantial costs (or the possibilities of large losses) would not occur until the private rate of return could be increased sufficiently to make the venture worthwhile. To illustrate the point: an improvement in a manufacturing process might occur by accident or by trial and error, but no 'research' would be undertaken as long as the benefits from such an improvement were immediately available to all other manufacturers and the costs of research were greater than that manufacturer's private gains from it. However, the ability to keep the improvement secret or to maintain a monopoly or exclusive patent rights would so increase the potential private profits that much higher research costs could be undertaken and the improvement would occur at an earlier time.[4] Innovation involving signifi-

---

[4] A logical corollary of this model is that where the nature of the industry prevents the private innovator from capturing a larger share of the social rate of return by secrecy, monopoly or patents, that industry's productivity gain will occur at a much slower pace than in

cant research costs would seldom, if ever, be worth the risk without some form of protection to internalize a significant share of its gains.

Innovation will be encouraged by modifying the institutional environment, so that the private rate of return approaches the social rate of return. Prizes and awards provide incentives for specific inventions, but do not provide a legal basis for ownership of intellectual property. The development of patent laws provides such protection. The forms of organization that have emerged since the end of the Middle Ages have evolved to encourage this internalization, so that the potential social rate of return can be realized by groups or individuals. The development of these organizational forms in the context of imperfect factor and product markets has resulted in the evolution of a system of property rights to define the gains from innovation and to see that they accrue to the individuals who undertake such innovation.

VI

Over the seventeenth century therefore we see the creation of the first patent law to encourage innovation; the elimination of many of the remnants of feudal servitude, with the Statute of Tenures; the burgeoning of the joint stock company, replacing the old regulated company; the development of the coffee house, which was a precursor of organized insurance; the creation of securities and commodity markets; the development of the goldsmith into a deposit banker issuing bank notes, discounting bills and providing interest on deposits; and the creation of a central bank, with the chartering of the Bank of England in 1694. Between 1688 and 1695 the number of joint stock companies increased from 22 to 150. The trading sector grew large enough to employ efficiently the commercial techniques adopted earlier by the Dutch.

By 1700 the institutional framework of England provided a hospitable environment for growth. The decay of industrial regulation and the declining power of guilds permitted mobility of labor and innovation in economic activity; this was later further encouraged by the Statute of Monopolies patent law. The mobility of capital was encouraged by joint stock companies, goldsmiths, coffee houses and the Bank of England, all of which lowered transaction costs in the capital market; and, perhaps most important, the supremacy of parliament and the embedding of property rights in the common law put political power in the hands of men anxious to exploit the new economic opportunities and provided the essential

---

other industries where the gains can be internalized. Agriculture was a specific case in point until the twentieth century, when the government systematically undertook the research.

framework for a judicial system to protect and encourage productive economic activity.

England, after an inauspicious start, by 1700 was experiencing sustained economic growth. It had developed an efficient set of property rights embedded in the common law. Besides the removal of hindrances to the allocation of resources both in the factor and product markets, England had begun to protect private property in knowledge with its patent law. The stage was now set for the industrial revolution.

EPILOGUE

This book ends where most studies of European economic development begin – in the eighteenth century. By that time a structure of property rights had developed in the Netherlands and England which provided the incentives necessary for sustained growth. These included the inducements required to encourage innovation and the consequent industrialization. The industrial revolution was not the source of modern economic growth. It was the outcome of raising the private rate of return on developing new techniques and applying them to the production process.

Moreover, international competition provided a powerful incentive for other countries to adapt their institutional structures to provide equal incentives for economic growth and the spread of the 'industrial revolution'. Success has been a consequence of the reorganization of property rights in those countries. The failures – the Iberian Peninsula in the history of the Western World, and much of Latin America, Asia and Africa in our times – have been a consequence of inefficient economic organization.

There is little new about this conclusion. Karl Marx and Adam Smith both subscribed to this view. They both saw successful growth as dependent on the development of efficient property rights. Their followers appear in the main to have forgotten this.

It would be wrong and misleading to end by agreeing unequivocally with either of the intellectual precursors of modern economic thought. Karl Marx was a utopian. He held that the world was going to progress through successive stages to Communism; capitalism required the development of efficient property rights, to make it the remarkable engine of progress which was necessary for this process.

Adam Smith inveighed against mercantilism and the inefficiencies of government. He also recognized that at times there were differences between private and social returns and that some essential functions require government.

However, Marx failed to recognize that there is nothing inevitable about economic growth and Smith did not tell us how to ensure an efficient government that will devise and maintain a set of property rights that assures sustained economic growth. We are just beginning to study economic organization and if this book encourages or provokes scholars and other students to take up the challenge, it will have accomplished its objective and converted our epilogue to a prologue.

BIBLIOGRAPHY

Chapter 1

An earlier condensed version of the theme of this book is presented in Douglass C. North and Robert Paul Thomas, 'An Economic Theory of the Growth of the Western World', *The Economic History Review*, 2nd series, 22, no. 1 (1970), 1–17.

The intellectual origins of the theory set out in this chapter can be traced to W. F. Baumol, *Welfare Economics and the Theory of the State* (Longmans, 1952); Anthony Downs, *An Economic Theory of Democracy* (Harper and Row, 1957); J. Buchanan and G. Tullock, *The Calculus of Consent* (University of Michigan, 1962); Harold Demsetz, 'Towards a Theory of Property Rights', *American Economic Review* (proceedings, May 1967); Kenneth Arrow, 'Political and Economic Evaluation of Social Effects and Externalities', Universities National Bureau Conference on the Economics of Public Output (unpublished, cited by permission of the author). Also see Joseph Schumpeter, 'The Crisis of the Tax State', *International Economic Papers*, no. 4 (1918), 5–38, and Frederic C. Lane, 'Economic Consequences of Organized Violence', *The Journal of Economic History*, 18, no. 4 (December 1958), 401–17.

Marxist historians have been concerned with the growth of the Western World. Maurice Dobb's *Studies in the Development of Capitalism* (International Publishers, 1946) provides an interesting account. See also Dobb's exchange with Paul Sweezy in *Science and Society*, no. 2 (1950), 134–67.

Chapter 2

The North–Thomas article cited above, 'An Economic Theory of the Growth of the Western World', provides a brief overview of the period under study. B. H. Slicher van Bath, *The Agrarian History of Western Europe; A.D. 500–1850* (Edward Arnold, 1963), surveys the history of the agricultural sector.

Chapter 3

A more detailed statement of the theory presented in this chapter is presented in Douglass C. North and Robert Paul Thomas, 'The Rise and Fall of the Manorial System: a Theoretical Model', *The Journal of Economic History*, 31, no. 4 (December 1971), 777–803; also see Evsey Domar, 'The Causes of Slavery or Serfdom: A Hypothesis', *The Journal of Economic History*, 30, no. 1 (March 1970).

Also see Steven N. S. Cheung, *The Theory of Share Tenancy* (University of Chicago Press, 1969), and 'The Structure of a Contract and the Theory of a Non-Exclusive Resource', *The Journal of Law and Economics*, 13 (April 1970), 49–70, for an analysis of the economics of modern agricultural controls.

Chapter 4

Henri Pirenne's views on medieval history are to be found mainly in his *Mohammed and Charlemagne* (Allen and Unwin, 1939); *Medieval Cities* (Princeton University Press, 1925); and *Economic and Social History of Medieval Europe* (Harcourt-Brace, 1956). The basis for the Marxian view is expressed in Karl Marx, introduction to *A Contribution to the Critique of Political Economy* (Charles H. Kerr and Co., 1904); also F. Engels, *Origin of the Family, Private Property, and the State* (International Publishers, 1942). The best exposition of the Marxist approach is contained in V. G. Childe, *History* (Corbett Press, 1947); the origins and early development of feudalism in England are described from a Marxist point of view in M. Gibbs, *Feudal Order* (Corbett Press, 1944), the Marxist point of view is also represented in M. Dobb, *Studies in the Development of Capitalism* (George Routledge and Sons, 1946).

A good summary of the exposed defects in the Pirenne thesis is found in A. Riising, 'The Fate of Henri Pirenne's Thesis on the Consequences of Islamic Expansion', *Classica et Medievalia*, 13 (1952).

Our description of the medieval countryside and the manor is based upon Georges Duby, *Rural Economy and Country Life in the Medieval West* (University of South Carolina Press, 1968); H. S. Bennett, *Life on the English Manor* (Macmillan, 1938); Doris Mary Stenton, *English Society in the Early Middle Ages, 1066–1307* (Penguin Books, 1951); H. L. Gray, *The English Field System* (Harvard, 1915); C. S. Orwin, *The Open Fields* (Clarendon Press, 1967) and *A History of English Farming* (Thomas Nelson and Sons, 1949); T. A. M. Bishop, 'Assarting and the Growth of the Open Fields', *The Economic History Review*, 6 (1935); Marc Bloch, *Feudal Society* (University of Chicago Press, 1961); Paul Vinogradoff, *Villeinage in England* (Clarendon Press, 1892); and *The Cambridge Economic History*, 2nd ed., vol. 1.

The free rider problem is mentioned in the text; for a contemporary complaint about this problem, see *Walter of Henley's Husbandry Together with an Anonymous Husbandry*, ed. E. Lamond (Royal Historical Society, 1890).

Our description of feudalism and the nature of land ownership is based upon D. R. Denman, *Origins of Ownership* (Allen and Unwin, 1958); J. J. Lawler and G. C. Lawler, *A Short Historical Introduction to the Law of Real Property* (Foundation Press, 1946); and Marshall Harris, *Origin of the Land Tenure System in the United States* (Iowa State College Press, 1953).

The explanation for the contractual form employed in the manor is presented in more detail in Douglass C. North and Robert Paul Thomas, 'The Rise and Fall of the Manorial System'.

Chapter 5

The citations listed in the bibliography to Chapter 4 for the medieval countryside and manor were also employed in writing this chapter plus the following: A. E. Levett, *Studies in Manorial History* (The Clarendon Press, 1938); R. H. Hilton, *A Medieval Society* (Weidenfeld and Nicolson, 1966); Warren C. Scoville and J. Clayburn LaForce, *The Middle Ages and the Renaissance* (D. C. Heath, 1969); B. H. Slicher Van Bath, *The Agrarian History of Western Europe: A.D. 500–1850*; Reginald Lennard, *Rural England, 1086–1135* (Clarendon Press, 1959); and J. Z. Titow, *English Rural Society, 1200–1350* (Allen and Unwin, 1969).

The awakening of trade and commerce and the beginnings of urbanization are aptly described in R. S. Lopez, 'The Trade of Medieval Europe in the South', *Cambridge Economic History*, vol. 2 (1952) and M. M. Postan, 'The Trade of Medieval Europe: The North', *Cambridge Economic History*, vol. 2.

A description of new technologies that were introduced during this period is found in Lynn White, Jr., *Medieval Technology and Social Change* (Clarendon Press, 1962). For a general discussion of the evolution of field systems see H. L. Gray, *English Field Systems*; C. S. Orwin, *The Open Fields* and *A History of English Farming*; also White, *Medieval Technology and Social Change*. For the best discussion of changing contractual arrangements see M. M. Postan, 'The Chronology of Labour Services', *Transactions of the Royal Historical Society*, 4th series, 20 (1937). Professor Postan covers the same subject in 'The Rise of a Money Economy', *The Economic History Review*, 14 (1944). Earlier contributions to the commutation debate can best be studied in the following: T. W. Page, *The End of Villeinage in England* (Macmillan, 1900); H. L. Gray, 'The Commutation of Villein Services in England before the Black Death', *The Economic History Review*, 29; E. A. Kosminsky, 'Services and Money Rents in the Thirteenth Century', *The Economic History Review*, 5, no. 2. For a discussion of assarting see D. M. Stenton, *English Society in the Middle Ages* and Paul Vinogradoff, *Villeinage in England*.

Georges Duby, in *Rural Economy and Country Life in the Medieval West* has an excellent description of colonization and its associated problems. H. S. Bennett, in *Life on the English Manor* has a good description of the evolution of the 'custom of the manor', pp. 99–101, which can be adequately supplemented by Marc Bloch, *Feudal Society*, pp. 113–16. Bloch in *Feudal Society* suggests that 'memory was the sole guardian of tradition' (p. 113). Bennett in *Life on the English Manor* also emphasizes the importance of the 'dooms' or the judgements of the jury in the manor court. For a description of differences in manorial structure see Duby, *Rural Economy and Country Life in the Medieval West*, pp. 47–54. Also see Chapter 29 of *Feudal Society* where Bloch compares the feudal systems of France, Germany and England, and *Cambridge Economic History of Europe*, 2nd ed., vol. 1, pp. 238–46.

The three-field system was called 'the greatest agricultural novelty of the Middle Ages' by C. Parain in *Cambridge Economic History*, vol. 1 (1941), p. 127, but White, *Medieval Technology and Social Change*, is perhaps the most oft-quoted source on the productivity gains to be had from the three-field technique. White, p. 74, also has a short discussion of the varying degrees of adaptations. Titow in *English Rural Society, 1200–1350*, p. 40, dismisses ignorance as the reason for non-adoption and accepts Gray's (*English Field Systems*) conclusion that soil conditions were the determining factor (pp. 71–3). Orwin, *A History of English Farming*, attributes the evolution of three course rotation mainly to population pressure and the need for more food (p. 13). Stenton in *English Society in the Middle Ages* blames 'a conservative adherence to the two-field system' (pp. 125–6).

For a summary of the sources of many technological advances see White, *Medieval Technology and Social Change* and 'The Medieval Roots of Modern Technology and Science', in Warren C. Scoville and J. Clayburn LaForce (eds), *The Economic Development of Western Europe* vol. 1 (Heath, 1969) and reprinted from Katherine F. Drew and Floyd S. Lear (eds.), *Perspectives in Medieval History* (University of Chicago, 1963). Also see A. P. Usher, *A History of Mechanical Inventions* (Harvard University Press, 1954), Chapter 7.

Chapter 6

There are a large number of local and regional monographs which do provide discrete statistics and regional time series but the generalized inferences one can draw are limited and controversial. On demographic material we have used Russell's *British Medieval Population*, though cautioned by Goran Ohlin's sobering comments on demographic history in Henry Rosovsky (ed.), *Industrialization in Two Systems; Essays in Honor of Alexander Gerschenkron* (Wiley, 1966). The urban population data come from *Cambridge Economic History*, vol. 3, p. 38. Another source of demographic data is Pollard and Crossley, *The Wealth of Britain, 1085–1966* (Schocken Books, 1969) and Henri Pirenne in 'The Place of the Netherlands in the Economic History of Medieval Europe', *The Economic History Review*, 2 (1929–50) discusses the urban character of the late medieval 'low countries'.

For price history we have relied on Pollard and Crossley; B. H. Slicher van Bath, *The Agrarian History of Western Europe; A.D. 500–1850*; D. L. Farmer, 'Grain Price Movements in Thirteenth Century England', *The Economic History Review*, 2nd series, 10 (1957–8); J. Z. Titow, *English Rural Society, 1200–1350*; William Abel, 'Agriculture and History', *International Encyclopedia of the Social Sciences* (Macmillan, 1968), vol. 5.

For much of the institutional description we have relied on *Cambridge Economic History*, vol. 3, particularly the essays on the organization of trade and on governments and public credit. Also see A. P. Usher, 'The Origins of Banking; The Primitive Bank of Deposits 1200–1600', *The Economic History Review*, 4 (1934) and J. A. Van Houtte, 'The Rise and Decline of the Market of Bruges', *The Economic History Review* (April 1966), pp. 29–48.

The growth of commercial law is discussed in Pollock and Maitland, Chapter 5. European commercial law is examined in Monroe Smith, *The Development of European Law* (Columbia Press, 1928). For a summary of the literature on English land law see North and Thomas, 'The Rise and Fall of the Manorial System', section 5.

Chapter 7

The information on the population movements of these centuries is as conjectural as for the earlier period. We usually know the direction, but both the magnitude and turning points are in dispute. In addition to the Bennett and Russell citations in the text many of the regional studies of the French sixth section explore demographic data including Pierre Vilar, *La Catalogue dans l'Espagne Moderne*, 3 vols. (Sevpen, 1962) and LeRoi La Durie, *Les Paysans de Languedoc* (Sevpen, 1964). Specialized studies abound, including J. M. W. Bean, 'Plague, Population, and Economic Decline in England in the Later Middle Ages', *The Economic History Review*, 2nd series, 15 (1963); D. Herlihy, 'Population, Plague and Social

Bibliography

Change in Rural Pistoria; 1261–1430', *The Economic History Review*, 2nd series, 18 (1965); M. M. Postan, 'Some Economic Evidence of Declining Population in the Later Middle Ages', *The Economic History Review*, 2nd series, 2 (1950). See also J. Hirshleifer, *Disaster and Recovery: The Black Death in Western Europe* (The Rand Corporation, 1966) for an economic analysis of the data. Price and wage data are contained in Slicher van Bath and M. M. Postan, 'The Fifteenth Century', *The Economic History Review*, 2nd series, 2 (1945–50).

For trade studies, see *Cambridge Economic History*, vol. 2; H. Miskemin, and the Vilar and LeRoi La Durie studies mentioned above. On the wool cloth trade see E. M. Carus-Wilson, 'Trends in the Export of English Woolens in the Fourteenth Century', *The Economic History Review*, 2nd series, 3 (1950).

The decline of serfdom is described in J. M. W. Bean, 'The Decline of Serfdom', *Cambridge Economic History*, vol. 1 (2nd ed.); North and Thomas, 'The Rise and Fall of the Manorial System'.

Changes in warfare as well as studies of the rise of nation states are described in C. W. Previte-Orton and Z. N. Brooke (eds.), *The Cambridge Medieval History*, vol. 8, *The Close of the Middle Ages* (Cambridge University Press, 1969). See also C. W. Previte-Orton's shorter version in *The Cambridge Shorter Medieval History*, vol. 2.

French fiscal policy is admirably examined in the forthcoming study of Martin Wolfe, *The Fiscal System of Renaissance France* (Yale University Press, 1972) Eileen Powes, *The Wool Trade in English Medieval History* (Clarendon Press, 1941) gives an excellent account of its role in English fiscal history. See also Stubbs (cited in text). The Burgundian rule in the Netherlands is described in Previte-Orton, *The Cambridge Shorter Medieval History*, and for Spain see Jaime Vincens Vives, *An Economic History of Spain* (Princeton University Press, 1969).

Chapter 8

The argument that the largest potential source of productivity gain during the early modern period was in the transactions sector is expanded in Clyde G. Reed, 'Transaction Costs and Differential Growth in Western Europe during the Seventeenth Century', *The Journal of Economic History* (forthcoming). Some of the ideas presented in this chapter were anticipated by Joseph Schumpeter, 'The Crisis of the Tax State' and by F. C. Lane in 'The Economic Consequences of Organized Violence'. The view that transactions are subject to economies of scale is suggested by Kenneth Arrow, 'Political and Economic Evaluation of Social Effects and Externalities'; and by Yoram Barzel, 'Investment, Scale and Growth', *Journal of Political Economy* (March–April 1971).

Chapter 9

The debate among Marxist historians as to how to interpret the early modern period is characterized by the Dobb–Sweezy controversy cited above. Also see E. J. Hobsbawm, 'The Crisis of the Seventeenth Century', *Past and Present*, nos. 5 and 6 (1954). The historical data on population for this period are summarized by Karl F. Helleiner in 'The Population of Europe from the Black Death to the Eve of the Vital Revolution', *Cambridge Economic History*, vol. 4. The figures for English population growth are those of J. Rickman, 'Estimated Population of England and Wales, 1570–1750', (Great Britain: Population Enumeration Abstract, 1843).

The history of prices for the early modern period owes much to Earl J. Hamilton whose two volumes on Spain during this period, *American Treasure and the Price Revolution in Spain, 1501–1650* (Octagon Books, 1965) and *War and Prices in Spain, 1651–1800* (Harvard University Press, 1947), contain a wealth of statistics. Hamilton is noted for his discovery of the inflation of the sixteenth century. Our knowledge of the price history of England and the Netherlands depends equally upon the work of Lord Beveridge, *Prices and Wages in England* (Longman, Green, 1936), and N. W. Posthumus, *Inquiry into the History of Prices in Holland*, 2 vols. (E. J. Brill, 1964). E. H. Phelps-Brown and Sheila V. Hopkins, in a series of articles cited in the text, summarized and organized the best series for English real wages and the terms of trade, as well as providing evidence for other countries. Eric Kerridge, 'The Movement of Rent, 1540–1640', *The Economic History Review* 2nd series, 6 (August 1953), provides the best information on the course of English money rents.

Chapter 10

A good summary of French economic history is to be found in Henri Hauser's 'The Characteristic Features of French Economic History from the Middle of the Sixteenth to the Middle of the Eighteenth Century', *The Economic History Review*, 4 (1933).

Our discussion of French fiscal history owes much to Martin Wolfe, *The Fiscal System of Renaissance France*. The agrarian history of France is summarized in Marc Bloch, *French Rural History* (University of California Press, 1966). We also consulted Abbott Payton Usher, *The History of the Grain Trade in France, 1400–1710* (Harvard University Press, 1913), Steven N. S. Cheung in *The Theory of Share Tenancy* cited above has a particularly valuable discussion of *metayage*. The history of industrial regulations in France is discussed in Eli Heckscher, *Mercantilism*, rev. ed., edited by E. F. Soderlund (Allen and Unwin, 1955) and in John U. Nef.

Industry and Government in France and England, 1540–1640 (Cornell University Press, 1957).

A summary of Spanish economic history is available in Vicens Vives, *An Economic History of Spain* and of Spanish political history in John Lynch, *Spain under the Hapsburgs*, 2 vols. (Blackwells, 1964, 1969). The definitive study of the Mesta is Julius Klein, *The Mesta* (Harvard University Press, 1920). The decline of Spain has received relatively much attention. See Earl J. Hamilton, 'The Decline of Spain', *The Economic History Review*, 8 (1938); J. H. Elliott, 'The Decline of Spain', *Past and Present*, 20 (November 1961), 52–73; and Maurice Schwarzmann, 'Background Factors in Spanish Economic Decline', *Explorations in Entrepreneural History*, 3 (1951), 221–47.

Chapter 11

Besides the works by Pirenne mentioned in the text, for the development of Dutch government and fiscal policy see H. G. Koenigsberger, 'The Estates General in the Netherlands Before the Revolt', in *Studies Presented to the International Commission for the History of Representative and Parliamentary Institutions*, 8 (no date). The expansion of the international market centered in the Low Countries is covered by any number of secondary sources, see the *Cambridge Economic History*, 4. The development of the Dutch fluteship is covered in Violet Barbour, 'Dutch and English Merchant Shipping in the Seventeenth Century', *The Economic History Review*, 2 (1930) and the same author's *Capitalism in Amsterdam During the Seventeenth Century* (Johns Hopkins Press, 1950) describes the rise of Amsterdam. Herman Van der Wee, *The Growth of the Antwerp Market and the European Economy* (Martinus Nijhoff, 1963) reviews the changes in commercial and agricultural organizations that occurred. For a description of these new crops and techniques see B. H. Slicher van Bath, 'The Rise of Intensive Husbandry in the Low Countries', in J. E. Bromley and E. H. Kossman (eds.), *Britain and the Netherlands* (Chatto and Windus, 1960).

Chapter 12

English political history is reviewed in W. C. Richardson, *Tudor Chamber Administration* (University of Louisiana Press, 1952); G. R. Elton, *The Tudor Revolution in Government* (Cambridge University Press, 1953); A. F. Pollard, *The Evolution of Parliament* (Longman, Green, 1926); and in *The Winning of the Initiative by the House of Commons* (Wallace Notestein, The British Academy, 1924) which provides a detailed description of the rise of the Commons in the early seventeenth century. The classic source on English public finance is F. C. Dïetz, *English Public Finance, 1558–1641*

(The Century Co., 1932). William Holdsworth, *Some Makers of English Law* (Cambridge University Press, 1966), lecture 6, provides a succinct discussion of Coke's role in English law and government, which summarizes his multi-volume history of English law. For a description of Coke's contribution see D. O. Wagner 'Coke and the Rise of Economic Liberalism', *The Economic History Review*, 6. The story of the rise of the chartered company is told in W. R. Scott, *Joint Stock Companies to 1720* (Cambridge University Press, 1912), vol. 1.

For a description of English agricultural change see Eric Jones, 'Agriculture and Economic Growth in England, 1660–1750', *The Journal of Economic History* (March 1965), 1–18. For a more detailed description of the trial-and-error process by which commons shifted to exclusive ownership and enclosure in Hampshire, see Bennett Baack, 'An Economic Analysis of the English Enclosure Movement' (unpublished PhD. dissertation, University of Washington, 1972). English industrial development is recounted in Eli Heckscher, *Mercantilism* and John U. Nef, *Industry and Government in France and England, 1540–1640*. For patents see Harold G. Fox, *Monopolies and Patents: A Study of the History and Future of the Patent Monopoly* (Toronto University Press, 1947). A partial list of the monopoly patent grants is given in E. W. Hulme, 'The Early History of the English Patent System', reprinted in *Selected Essays in Anglo-American Legal History* (Little Brown and Co., 1909), vol. 3.

INDEX

Index

innovation, commercial, 5, 135, 138, 140, 154, 155; *see also* technology, changes in

institutional arrangements: changes in agriculture, 51, 88; creation of new, 6, 51, 53, 138; customs of the manor, 5; influence on efficiency, 5, 6, 70

joint stock company: advantages of, 17; expansion of, 155; monopoly, 149, 154

just price, 92

justice: provision of on manor, 30, 65, 124; provision by nation states, 64, 124, 156; provision of in towns, 65

knights, *see* nobility

labor: of freemen, 64, 142; mobility of, 127, 134, 152; value of, 30, 75, 96; wages, 77, 116–19

land: copyhold, 80; development of private property, 64, 123, 142; growing scarcity, of, 42; life leases, 79; *metayage* (sharecropping), 124–5; rents, 77; stinting, 150

lords, *see* nobility

Magna Carta, 83, 96

Magyars, 11, 19, 29

Malthusian checks, 105, 115, 132; cycle, 102; pressure, 13; reaction, 16, 69; trap, 103

manor: contractual arrangements, 10–12, 38, 79; customs of, 11, 19, 20, 22, 23, 27, 38, 39, 61, 62, 80; decline of, 13, 87; definition of, 10; described, 27; lords of, *see* nobility; manorial court, 65; regulations, 19, (*see also* customs of); serfs, *see* serfdom

manorialism: changes in contractual arrangements, 38; explanation of, 13, 32

market economy, *see* trade

Marxian view, 25, 102, 157

Medici, 13, 76

Mesta, 4, 5, 85, 86, 88, 128, 129, 131

money: existence of money economy, 87; influence of money economy, 39

monopolies: created by government, 98–9, 123; *see also* government; guilds; patents

Moslem, 11, 19, 29

nation state: explanation for rise of, 95; fiscal crisis, 80–3; rise of, 80, 87–9, 95, 146; role of trade in creation, 94

Nef, J., 151

nobility: obligations of, 27; providers of protection, 19; rights of, 27; scutage, 35, 40, 65; social role of, 19

Norsemen, 11, 19, 29, 34

open fields: common fields, 26, 27, 151; costs of, 151; three-field, 34, 41, 42; two-field, 30, 43; *see also* common property

parliament, *see* government

patents: English, 147, 148, 152, 153; French, 126

peasant revolts, 73, 78, 81

pirates, 3, 5, 29, 34, 137

Pirenne, Henri, 25, 48, 132

plague, 13, 72, 78, 88, 104, 105, 118

population: decline of, 13, 24, 71–4, 76, 78, 86, 104, 118; determination of, 21, 70, 78; effect of, 21, 75, 115; increase, 11, 12, 13, 23, 26, 33, 35, 42, 47, 103, 105, 113; social costs of, 70; urban, 47

Postan, M. M., 48, 73

prices: absolute level of, 46, 48, 60, 74; definition, 74; inflation, 48, 49, 60, 106, 108, 113; relative, 12, 46, 48, 60, 74, 75, 77, 79, 108

productivity: of agriculture, 77; influence of specialization, 52, 59; of manufacturing, 77; *see also* diminishing returns to labor; institutional arrangements

property rights: creation of, 8, 18, 19, 67, 69, 70, 98, 141, 148; enforcement of, 5, 7, 67, 87, 133, 148, 155; evolution of, 16; feudal basis for land tenure, 28; influence upon economic organization, 3, 4, 7, 120; inheritance, 30; in land, right to transfer, 63; in man, 20; private property 133; role of government, 6, 18, 97, 98, 100, 133

public good: defined, 7n; example of, 27; provision of, 29, 30, 65

Russell, J. C., 71, 72, 73

scutage, 11

serfdom: change in contractual arrangement, 12, 39, 40, 59, 60, 92; decline of, 22, 35, 92, 143; effect upon productivity, 61; influence of market on, 20; obligations of, 10, 27, 60–2; reason for existence, 20, 21

serfs: obligations of, 10, 27, 60–2; rights of, 10, 27; *see also* serfdom

shipping: developments in navigation, 3; efficiency of Dutch, 149; flute ship, 137

slaves, reasons for disappearance of, 20

Smith, A., 157

standard of living, 12, 21, 23, 70, 77, 78, 88, 117–19

statutes: Artifices, 151; Labourers, 79; Merton, 63, 150; Monopolies, 148, 152, 154; Navigation Act, 149; *Quia emptores*,